The Joy of Ginger

A Winning Selection of Taste-Tingling Recipes

Margaret Conrad and Heather MacDonald

D0783353

NIMBUS
PUBLISHING LTD

Nimbus Publishing Limited
PO Box 9301, Station A
Halifax, Nova Scotia B3K 5N5
(902) 455-4286

Designer: Kathy Kaulbach, Halifax
Illustrations: Tatjana
Printed and bound in Canada

**Canadian Cataloguing in
Publication Data**
Conrad, Margaret.
The joy of ginger
Includes index.
ISBN 1-55109-198-4
1. Cookery (Ginger).
I. MacDonald, Heather.   II. Title
TX 819.G53C66 1997   641.6'383
C97-950025-7

To our mothers and grandmothers,
all gifted cooks, who prepared
thousands of meals for countless
hungry mouths and never lost their
love of the craft.

Contents
Contents
Contents
Contents
Contents
Contents
Contents
Contents

Recipes

Acknowledgements

Preparing this cookbook was a learning experience for both of us and we are indebted to many people for offering us help along the way. Professor Alison Bogan, School of Nutrition and Food Science, Acadia University, steered us in the right direction when we decided to do a nutritional analysis of our recipes. In addition to introducing us to Elizabeth Warwick's computer programs for nutrient analysis of recipes, she also suggested that we contact the Kentville Agricultural Centre, Agriculture Canada, where Jerry Miner, Regional Librarian, and Catherine Sanford, Biologist, Food Quality Research, were most helpful.

Elaine Elliott and Virginia Lee, who have several published cookbooks to their credit, offered us help and encouragement throughout the process. Jacquie Simes, Marketing Officer for Buderim Limited, showered us with recipes and information about ginger, checked our introductory remarks for accuracy, and even lent us a transparency of a ginger farm on the Sunshine Coast of Australia. We are grateful for her efforts on our behalf. Carroll Klein, a professional editor and fabulous cook, proofread the penultimate version of our manuscript and brought consistency to our prose. When we needed help at

the last minute, Dianne Looker graciously sacrificed her time and resources. Dorothy Blythe was a patient publisher and appreciative taste-tester. Without her enthusiastic support, this book would still be in the planning stage and *sans* title. Joanne Elliott, Paula Sarson, and Joan Sinclair saved us from many errors by their careful editorial work and patiently accepted all of our last minute changes. Many of our recipes came from friends and relatives who are acknowledged throughout the text. They suffered our failures as well as our successes in the kitchen and kept us honest.

Introduction

When we were young girls growing up in post-Second World War Nova Scotia, ginger figured prominently in our diets. Most Maritime pantries still included powdered, preserved, and candied gingers, which found their way into breads, pies, cakes, marmalades, and even baked beans. On special occasions, we were treated to Farmers' ginger ice cream and Moirs' ginger chocolates, both manufactured in Halifax. Ginger ale, bottled in various sites around the region—our favourite was the Sussex brand—invariably was prescribed as we convalesced from childhood diseases. In some homes, ginger concoctions, made from powdered ginger produced by Schwartz in Halifax or Barbours in Saint John, were administered to cure indigestion, cramps, and other stomach ailments.

Ginger has a long history and figures prominently in folklore. According to the Koran, ginger is included on the menu in Paradise. It was reputedly served to the Knights at King Arthur's Round Table. First grown in Asia, it was imported to Greece and Rome in small clay jars, much like the Chinese porcelain containers that can be found in specialty stores today. It is stretching the point only a little to suggest that the European "discovery" of the Americas was due in large measure to ginger. When the eastern route to the Orient was blocked by hostile forces in the fifteenth century, explorers sailed west in an effort to restore the trade in spices, which was vital to the European diet.

Many claims have been made for ginger over the years. While its value as a preservative and a digestive have stood the test of time and experience, views that it prolongs life, cures cancer, and increases one's sexual appetite continue to be called into question. In his book *Common Spice or Wonder Drug: Ginger Health Care Rediscovers its Roots,* Paul Schulick makes a good case for keeping an open mind on the medicinal qualities of ginger, and we are not surprised that progressive people in the scientific community are beginning to take ginger very seriously.

An underground stem of a tropical plant, ginger does not, of course, grow in the temperate climate of the Maritime Provinces of Canada. Nevertheless, it has a close association with the region. Dried ginger was used as a medicine, preservative, and sweet spice by immigrants from France and Great Britain, the two nations to which many people in the Maritimes trace their ancestry. Today, the spice racks in most supermarkets offer many choices to the adventurous chef, but until recently salt, pepper, and ginger were the dominant flavouring ingredients in Maritime cuisine. During the heyday of the age of sail, the Maritimes had easy access to supplies of ginger from the Caribbean and other ginger-growing areas of the world, which accounts for the manufacture of powdered ginger, ginger chocolates, ginger ale, and ginger ice cream in the region. Many collectors now pay premium prices for the ceramic ginger beer bottles that survive as a reminder of the many bottling plants that dotted the region in the latter half of the nineteenth century.

As children, we did not often encounter fresh ginger, but we developed a taste for the gnarled rhizome that favourably disposed us toward the ginger-flavoured African and Asian cuisines introduced into our culture in the sixties. Ironically, the sweet ginger delights on which we were raised began to fall out of fashion just as ginger-enhanced foods from around the world began to make our main courses more interesting. While we can now sample scrumptious pork with ginger at fine restaurants, it is increasingly difficult to buy ginger ice cream and ginger chocolates, once sold throughout the Maritimes. This unremarked loss of what we considered to be one of the more exotic features of our culinary heritage prompted Margaret in the early 1980s to collect ginger recipes and to think vaguely about publishing a cookbook devoted to ginger. In the fall of 1994, she mentioned the idea to Heather and it gradually became a reality. The recipes were tested after work on Friday evenings over a two-year period, which proved to be an inspired way to repair the ravages of the increasingly stressful work week and led to the diverse and delectable recipes found here.

The recipes included in this book were selected from a wide range of sources. We consulted the cookbooks on our kitchen shelves, turned to relatives and friends—many of whom had favourite ginger recipes both old and new—and even surfed the Net in pursuit of ginger. It was not long before we discovered Bruce Cost's *Ginger East to West,* which proved to be a valuable source. Some of our finest dinners came from this classic on the topic of ginger cookery—a copy should be found in every ginger-lover's library. For a British perspective on ginger, we found Brigid Allen's *Cooking with Garlic, Ginger & Chilies* and other Sainsbury publications very useful. *A Century of Canadian Home Cooking: 1900 Through the '90s* by Carol Ferguson and

Margaret Fraser led us to several cookbooks that were widely consulted in the Maritimes in the early years of this century.

During a visit to Australia in April 1996, Margaret discovered a ginger treasure trove: the Buderim Ginger Factory, in the Queensland town of Yandina. Reputedly the largest ginger production facility in the world, the Buderim Ginger Factory produces a wide range of ginger products and, not surprisingly, has its own publication titled the *Little Ginger Cookbook,* consisting of recipes gathered from its many customers. Judy Walker, Pamela King, and Olive Evans also published an Australian cookbook titled *Ginger for a Tropical Taste.* The popularity of ginger seems to be on the rise.

When it came time to make a selection from the hundreds of recipes we had gathered in our files, we decided to emphasize those containing enough ginger to "make a statement." Thus, readers will find that most recipes call for at least a tablespoon and some for as much as a cup and a half of fresh ginger. The only exceptions are traditional recipes that we felt should be preserved in their original form.

A nutritional analysis of our recipes revealed that some of them were high in fat and carbohydrates. While this was not a concern to our

grandmothers and many great chefs even today, it inspired us to publish a nutritional breakdown that we developed from Dr. Elizabeth Warwick's computerized Nutrient program (1994). Fortunately, ginger itself adds few calories and little fat to food. A half cup of grated ginger yields less than fifty calories and virtually no fat.

We are now so addicted to ginger that we tend to add more than the amount stated in the recipe, often doubling the quantity. Since ginger is an acquired taste, we leave it to the reader to decide how much ginger suits the palate. We can, however, state categorically that any food—with the possible exception of dulse—benefits from a generous dollop of fresh ginger.

In the process of testing our recipes, we altered each of them in some way or other, but we have made every effort to credit the source of our inspiration. We encourage readers to experiment with alternative ingredients, except, of course, the ginger, which is essential to every recipe in this book!

About Ginger

Ginger is not a root but a rhizome, a tuber-like stem that grows best in tropical countries with rich, sandy soil and hot, humid climates. It is closely related to turmeric and galangal, which, like ginger, come from the *Zingiberaceae* family of plants. Cardamoms are the seed pods of several species of ginger. Although China and India raise the bulk of the world's commercial ginger crop, North Americans also buy ginger from Australia, Hawaii, Fiji, Jamaica, and South America, especially Brazil. The flavour of the ginger differs depending upon where it is grown, but any source is fine as long as the product is fresh.

Until recently, good fresh ginger was difficult to find in most Canadian grocery stores. Consumers still need to guard against shrivelled or mouldy knobs that are passed off as fresh ginger. Do not settle for second best. When shopping for ginger, look for hard "hands" (the shape of ginger resembles a human hand, hence the term) with smooth, unblemished brown skin. "Young" ginger is sweeter and less fibrous than "old," but the mature variety is usually more flavourful. For recipes calling for a fine mince, young ginger is easier to work

A field of ginger. Photo courtesy of Buderim Ginger Limited.

with. Ginger well past its prime is dry and loses its flavour. Throw it away.

Store ginger unwrapped in the crisper of your refrigerator if you plan to use it immediately. Otherwise, to guard against the moisture that causes mildew, wrap it in a paper towel and put in a plastic bag before refrigeration. Use it within two or three weeks. Do not freeze ginger unless you cannot buy it regularly; frozen ginger turns to mush and can be used only for recipes calling for juiced or blended ginger. We tend to make ginger sauce from ginger that has reached the end of its lifespan. Others dry it by leaving it in the sun for ten days or in a commercial dryer, to be ground into powder in a spice grinder, as required.

Unless you are using very

young ginger or making ginger sauce or other recipes in which the ginger juice is strained out, it should be peeled with a sharp knife or scraped with the edge of a spoon to remove the tough outer layer. Knobs and small branches should be removed for use in chops or minces.

To secure the best flavour and texture from fresh ginger, it is important to develop the proper skills of slicing, shredding, chopping, mincing, grating, smashing, juicing, and pounding the tough little rhizome. Margaret argues that life is too short for such time-consuming activities and therefore tends to use only grated fresh ginger, but Heather agrees with all good chefs that the subtle differences in ginger preparation are crucial to the success of the recipe.

Ginger Vocabulary

Chop: Cut slivers into lengths desired, and then into 1/4-inch (1 cm) width for most recipes.

Grate: There are Japanese graters called *oroshigane,* made especially for ginger. Buy one or use the fine holes in a Western grater. The chopping mode in a blender also produces a similar effect and saves a lot of time. Whatever method is used, save and use the juice.

Juice: Grate very fresh ginger onto a cheesecloth, wrap the cloth around the ginger and squeeze. Another method is to press the grated ginger against a fine tea strainer. It is also possible to produce a flavourful juice by pouring boiling water over ginger peelings. Juice so produced will last a week or so stored in a jar in the refrigerator. Ginger juice separates into liquid on the top and a starch that settles to the bottom. The liquid tastes slightly bitter on its own but is sweet and delicious when combined with the starch. Your finger is the best tool for stirring the two together.

Mince: Chop the slivers even more finely. You need a very sharp knife for this skill-testing activity. Another approach is to smash a peeled ginger knob with the side of a knife and chop finely.

Pound: Most people use a blender to accomplish what used to be done by a mortar and pestle, that is, pound fresh ginger with other ingredients to make an aromatic paste used in Asian and Indian cuisines. Either way works well.

Slice: Slice ginger across the fibres as thinly as possible to produce very thin slivers.

Sliver: Cut the ginger lengthwise on the oval into long, very thin strips or stack ovals of thinly sliced ginger and cut into fine slivers.

Smash: Peel a small knob or take a slice of ginger 1/4-inch (1 cm) thick and smash it with a knife or garlic press.

Ginger Measurements

Most ginger pieces are about 1 inch (2.5 cm) thick and many recipes call for a piece of ginger of varying lengths. As a rule of thumb, the following measurements of an average piece of ginger will yield the following:

**2 inches of fresh ginger =
3 tbsp (45 mL), finely chopped**

**4 inches of fresh ginger =
1/2 cup (125 mL), finely chopped**

**6 inches of fresh ginger =
2/3 cup (175 mL), finely chopped**

**8 inches of fresh ginger =
1 cup (250 mL), finely chopped**

Although Canada has used the metric system since 1972, the imperial system remains popular. In deference to users of each, we include both systems of measurement. You can expect a slight variation between the results of one system and the other.

Ginger Syrup

An essential ingredient in every cook's kitchen, this pungent syrup can be added to many dessert recipes with wonderful results and makes a fabulous flavouring for whipped cream. On cold winter nights a few tablespoons of ginger syrup added to warm milk makes a divine Ginger Cream (see page 6).

1 cup	grated ginger	250 mL
2 cups	brown sugar	500 mL
2 cups	water	500 mL

Mix sugar and ginger in a small saucepan. Cover with water and bring to a boil. Boil gently, uncovered, for 25 to 30 minutes. Add more water if necessary to prevent burning.

When the liquid has reduced to about two-thirds, remove from heat and press it through a sieve, squeezing as much juice and pulp into the liquid as possible.

The syrup can be stored covered in the refrigerator for 2 or more weeks.

Makes 1 1/2 cups

per serving (2 tbsp/30 mL)
calories 150
g fat 0.1
g fibre 0.4
calorie breakdown
% protein 0
% fat 0
% carbohydrate 99

Purists argue that to secure the maximum flavour it is essential to use a hand-operated food mill to process the syrup. At the very least, once the sauce is boiled it should be passed through a sieve and the remaining pulp rubbed through the mesh with a wooden spoon.

Ginger Tea

Many people spoke to us about having ginger tea as a nostrum for colds, arthritis, headaches, cramps, and other ailments. According to Headlines: Canada's Migraine Newsletter *(compliments of Liz Ramscar), migraine sufferers "drink ginger tea during migraine attacks to ease the pain and counter the nausea."*

No. 1

1 tbsp	grated ginger	15 mL
1 tbsp	honey	15 mL
1 tsp	grated lemon zest	5 mL
2 cups	boiling water	500 mL

✎ Add ginger, honey, and lemon to boiling water. Steep for 5 minutes. Strain into heated cup and serve.

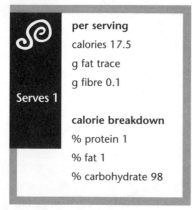

per serving
calories 17.5
g fat trace
g fibre 0.1

Serves 1

calorie breakdown
% protein 1
% fat 1
% carbohydrate 98

No. 2

4 cups	water	1 L
2 tbsp	coarsely grated ginger	30 mL
1	lemon	1
1 tbsp	honey	15 mL

✎ Put water, ginger, lemon, and honey in a saucepan, bring to a boil, and simmer for about 15 minutes. Remove lemon, slice in half, and add juice to the saucepan ingredients. Add more honey, if desired, strain and serve in a heated mug.

per serving
calories 21.4
g fat trace
g fibre 0.1

Serves 4

calorie breakdown
% protein 2
% fat 1
% carbohydrate 97

Both of these recipes make a good iced drink in summer and a good cold remedy when laced with rum or brandy.

Ginger-infused coffee can be made by substituting ginger tea (made without honey and lemon) for water when you brew your next cup of coffee. Since the ginger tea may leave an aftertaste in your coffee maker, it is best to use a filter or Bodum coffee maker for this recipe.

Ginger Lemonade

Adapted from *A Treasury of Nova Scotia Heirloom Recipes*

This drink was reputedly popular at haying time because of its thirst-quenching properties and refreshing tang.

1/2 cup	vinegar	125 mL
1 cup	sugar	250 mL
2 tsp	ginger powder	10 mL
3 cups	ice water	750 mL
1 tsp	soda	5 mL

Mix vinegar, sugar, and ginger in a 1-qt (1 L) pitcher. Fill with ice water. Add 1 tsp (5 mL) soda to make the mixture fizz.

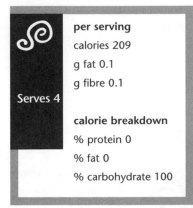

per serving
calories 209
g fat 0.1
g fibre 0.1

Serves 4

calorie breakdown
% protein 0
% fat 0
% carbohydrate 100

Tropical Punch

In response to our request for recipes over the Internet, JoAnne Cornwall, who works at the University of Texas Health Science Centre, sent us this winner for a punch worthy of any occasion, casual or formal. JoAnne found this gem in a grocery store brochure.

1/4 cup	chopped ginger	50 mL
3 cups	water	750 mL
2 cups	sugar	500 mL
6-8	whole cloves	6-8
12 oz	frozen orange juice	355 mL
12 oz	frozen apple juice	355 mL
2 1/2 cups	fresh lemon juice	625 mL
orange or apple slices		
whole cloves		

Combine ginger, water, sugar, and cloves; bring to a boil, then simmer for 5 minutes. Cool and allow mixture to steep for 6 to 8 hours.

Combine ginger mixture with orange and apple juices that have been diluted with water according to package directions, and the lemon juice. Strain mixture to remove ginger and fruit pulp.

To serve cold, pour over a block of ice in a punch bowl. On top, float orange slices studded with cloves.

To serve hot, warm just to steaming. Keep warm using a hot tray or place in a large, clean electric coffee maker. In each cup, float apple slices studded with cloves.

This punch can be spiked with rum or brandy for a lively twist.

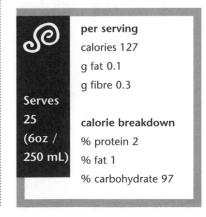

per serving
calories 127
g fat 0.1
g fibre 0.3

Serves 25 (6oz / 250 mL)

calorie breakdown
% protein 2
% fat 1
% carbohydrate 97

Ginger Sherry

A good substitute for ginger wine and a heart-warming drink on a cold winter's afternoon.

3 tbsp	grated ginger	45 mL
1(24-oz)	bottle dry or	
	medium dry sherry	750 mL

Add the ginger to the sherry and store for 1 or 2 days, until the flavour suffuses throughout. Someone once asked us if the ginger turned mouldy. Our bottle didn't last long enough for us to find out!

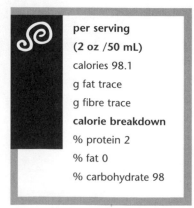

per serving	
(2 oz /50 mL)	
calories 98.1	
g fat trace	
g fibre trace	
calorie breakdown	
% protein 2	
% fat 0	
% carbohydrate 98	

Whisky Mac

This fine medicinal remedy, recommended to us by Dr. Mary Roddis, who grew up in Scotland, is a soothing variation on a Rusty Nail. According to Dr. Roddis, the quality of the Scotch is as important as the use of Stone's Original Green Ginger Wine in this remedy for any "illness."

1 1/2 oz	single malt Scotch	45 mL
1 1/2 oz	ginger wine	45 mL
2	ice cubes	

Combine the Scotch and ginger wine in an old-fashioned glass, add the ice cubes, and stir gently.

Serves 1

per serving
calories 168
g fat 0
g fibre 0
calorie breakdown
% protein 0
% fat 0
% carbohydrate 99

Presbyterian

There were many Presbyterians in Nova Scotia before they were caught up in the United Church, established in 1925. At the time, prohibition was in force and Presbyterians were strong supporters of the cause. If you are not a temperance advocate, add some bourbon.

2 to 3	ice cubes	
3 oz	bourbon (optional)	90 mL
2 oz	cold ginger ale	60 mL
2 oz	cold club soda	60 mL
1 strip	lemon zest	

Combine the ice cubes, bourbon, ginger ale, and club soda in a highball glass and stir. Twist the lemon zest over the glass to release its oil and drop it in.

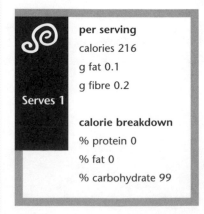

Serves 1

per serving
calories 216
g fat 0.1
g fibre 0.2
calorie breakdown
% protein 0
% fat 0
% carbohydrate 99

Moscow Mule

Ginger ale and ginger beer are popular in a variety of traditional mixed drinks such as this one. The ginger lends its distinctive flavour to make a pleasant drink.

2 or 3	ice cubes	
	lime juice to taste	
3 oz	vodka	90 mL
6 oz	cold ginger beer	180 mL
1 slice	lime	

🍥 Place the ice cubes in a beer mug or heavy glass and add the lime juice and vodka. Fill the mug or glass with ginger beer and top with a slice of lime.

🍥	**per serving**
	calories 263
	g fat trace
	g fibre 0.1
Serves 1	
	calorie breakdown
	% protein 0
	% fat 0
	% carbohydrate 99

Ginger Rum Toddy

Rum toddies are an effective long-standing remedy for colds and other ailments. This one is good even if you are in perfect health.

8 oz	fresh apple cider	250 mL
2 tbsp	dark rum	30 mL
1 tsp	ginger juice*	5 mL
	lime juice to taste	

*See page viii

🍥 Combine all ingredients and heat in the microwave for 2 minutes on high.

🍥	**per serving**
	calories 199
	g fat trace
	g fibre 0.1
Serves 1	
	calorie breakdown
	% protein 1
	% fat 0
	% carbohydrate 99

To make a milk-based rum toddy, stir 1 tsp (5 mL) each of sugar and ground ginger in a mug with 8 oz (250 mL) of hot milk. Top with a dollop of butter and a sprinkling of ground nutmeg.

The British produce an exotic elixir called the Kings Ginger Liqueur, which makes a perfect ending to any dinner party.

Ginger Cream

We keep a supply of ginger syrup (see page 1) in the refrigerator for this recipe, guaranteed to cure whatever ails you and to induce a sound night's sleep. This idea came to us from Toni Laidlaw, a psychologist in Halifax, Nova Scotia, who understands well the value of comfort food.

2 tbsp	ginger syrup or	
	more to taste	30 mL
1 cup	hot milk	250 mL

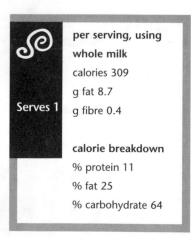 Mix ginger syrup in a cup of hot milk and enjoy.

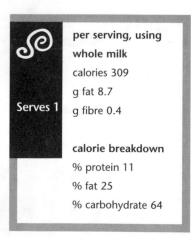	**per serving, using whole milk**
	calories 309
	g fat 8.7
Serves 1	g fibre 0.4
	calorie breakdown
	% protein 11
	% fat 25
	% carbohydrate 64

Real Ginger Beer

Adapted from Bruce Cost's
Ginger East to West

There are as many ginger beer recipes as there are beer makers. This one is especially good on a hot summer day.

1/4 cup	coarsely grated ginger,	
	with the juice	50 mL
grated zest of 2 limes		
6 tbsp	fresh lime juice	90 mL
1 cup	light brown sugar	250 mL
4 cups	boiling water	1 L
1 tsp	active dry yeast	5 mL
1/4 cup	lukewarm water	
	(110°F/40°C)	50 mL
1/4 cup	light rum or	
	more to taste	50 mL

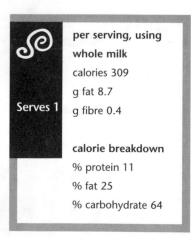 In a large ceramic bowl, combine the ginger, lime zest, lime juice, and sugar, and pour in the boiling water.

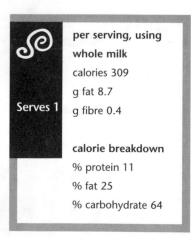 In a small bowl, sprinkle yeast over the lukewarm water and let stand 2 minutes; then stir yeast until completely dissolved. Set the bowl in a warm place until it begins to bubble, about 5 minutes. If it does not bubble, start over with fresh yeast.

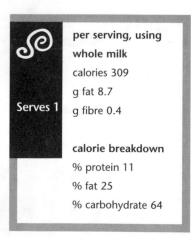 Add the yeast mixture to the ceramic bowl mixture, cover tightly with plastic wrap, and let stand for 1 week in a warm, draft-free spot. Stir briefly every other day. Add rum to mixture after 5 days.

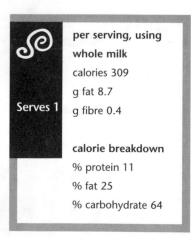 At the end of the week, strain the mixture into a 1-qt (1 L) glass or ceramic container and cork it. Allow to stand for 3 days at room temperature, then chill before serving. It is usually served over ice, with a slice of lime.

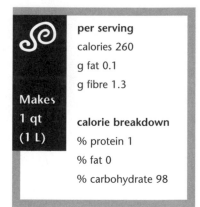	**per serving**
	calories 260
	g fat 0.1
	g fibre 1.3
Makes 1 qt (1 L)	
	calorie breakdown
	% protein 1
	% fat 0
	% carbohydrate 98

Make a Boston Cooler by putting a scoop of vanilla ice cream in a glass of dry ginger ale.

Condiments
Condiments
Condiments
Condiments
Condiments
Condiments
Condiments
Condiments

Spicy Ginger Oil

The spicy oils found in gourmet shops are easy and inexpensive to make. We use this one in salad dressings or to give pastas and stir-frys a flavour boost.

2 inches	ginger,	
	thinly sliced	5 cm
4	small dried chilies	4
2 tbsp	coriander seeds	30 mL
1 tbsp	black peppercorns	15 mL
1 tbsp	juniper berries	15 mL
1	cinnamon stick	1
1 1/2 cups canola oil		375 mL

🍥 Fill a sterilized (and if possible decorative) bottle with ginger and spices. Add canola oil, seal, and store for 1 or 2 weeks before using. Keep in a dark, cool place.

🍥	per tablespoon
	calories 129
	g fat 14.5
	g fibre trace
Makes	
1 1/2	**calories**
cups	% protein 0
(375 mL)	% fat 99
	% carbohydrate 1

Herbed Ginger Vinegar

One of the best and easiest ways we know to create a splendid salad dressing is to combine a spiced oil with a herbed vinegar—both, of course, laced with ginger. Try this recipe or experiment with your own herbed vinegar, using about 1 cup (250 mL) of herbs to 4 cups (1 L) of vinegar.

3	sprigs parsley	3
2	sprigs sage	2
2	sprigs rosemary	2
2	sprigs thyme	2
2 inches	ginger, thinly sliced	5 cm
4 cups	apple cider vinegar	1 L

🍥 Loosely fill a sterilized bottle with herbs and ginger. Add vinegar. After sealing and labelling the bottle let it stand in a cool, dark place for at least 3 to 4 weeks. Check the bottle after a few days to make sure that the herbs are still covered by the vinegar, adding more vinegar if needed and resealing. Handle the bottle carefully to avoid disturbing the infusion. Use the vinegar within 1 year.

🍥	per tablespoon
	calories 2.4
	g fat trace
	g fibre trace
Makes	
4 cups	**calories**
(1 L)	% protein 1
	% fat 0
	% carbohydrate 99

Ginger Marinades

Ginger is almost a necessity in marinades used to flavour meat and fish before grilling. These recipes were suggested to us by Jacqueline Simes, marketing officer, Buderim Ginger Limited in Yandina. The Australians really know how to barbecue.

Ginger Soy Marinade

Here is an all-purpose marinade that compliments just about anything.

1/3 cup	soy sauce	90 mL
2 tbsp	lime juice	30 mL
1 tbsp	honey	15 mL
2 tbsp	grated ginger	30 mL

Mix all ingredients together and use to marinate steak, ribs, chicken, fish, pork, or burgers for 2 to 3 hours before broiling.

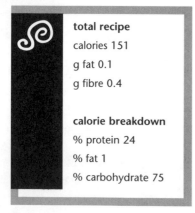

total recipe
calories 151
g fat 0.1
g fibre 0.4

calorie breakdown
% protein 24
% fat 1
% carbohydrate 75

Ginger Horseradish Chicken Marinade

This tangy chicken marinade will win rave reviews.

2 tsp	grated ginger	10 mL
1 clove	garlic, crushed	1 clove
2 tsp	horseradish	10 mL
1/2 cup	white wine	125 mL
2 tsp	salt	10 mL
2 tbsp	honey	30 mL
freshly ground black pepper		

Mix all ingredients together. Pour over chicken breasts and leave in refrigerator overnight before baking or barbecuing.

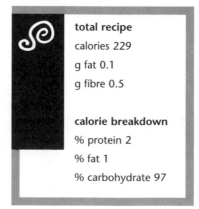

total recipe
calories 229
g fat 0.1
g fibre 0.5

calorie breakdown
% protein 2
% fat 1
% carbohydrate 97

Ginger Mustard Pork Marinade

Dinner guests will beg to be invited back for this delectable combination of ginger and mustard with pork.

1/4 cup	raspberry vinegar	75 mL
2 tsp	Dijon mustard	10 mL
2 tbsp	grated ginger,	
	finely chopped	30 mL
1/4 cup	white wine	75 mL
1/4 cup	corn syrup	75 mL

Mix all the ingredients, pour over loin or fillet of pork and leave in refrigerator overnight before roasting or barbecuing.

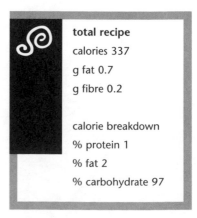

total recipe
calories 337
g fat 0.7
g fibre 0.2

calorie breakdown
% protein 1
% fat 2
% carbohydrate 97

Ginger Lemon Yogurt Dip/Salad Dressing

This versatile recipe for dip or dressing takes a hit of ginger without any complaint. We initially served it with zucchini coins, but it goes well with any raw or lightly steamed fresh vegetables, such as carrots, peppers, and broccoli.

6 tbsp	low-fat yogurt	90 mL
6 tbsp	cream cheese	90 mL
2 tsp	grated ginger	10 mL
1/2 tsp	horseradish	2 mL
zest of 2 lemons		
1 tbsp	fresh dill	15 mL

🌀 Mix all ingredients except dill in a bowl or blender. Add dill and mix to combine.

Note: *By adding more yogurt, this recipe also serves as a tasty salad dressing.*

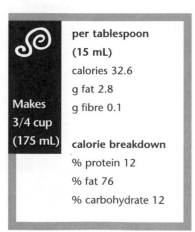

🌀 Makes 3/4 cup (175 mL)	per tablespoon (15 mL) calories 32.6 g fat 2.8 g fibre 0.1 **calorie breakdown** % protein 12 % fat 76 % carbohydrate 12

Spicy Peanut Sauce

This delicious sauce makes a pleasing complement as a dip, a salad dressing, or a sauce for barbecued chicken. Once you've tried it, you'll be hooked on the nutty flavour.

2 tbsp	coarsely chopped onion	30 mL
1 large	garlic clove, coarsely chopped	1
1 tbsp	grated ginger	15 mL
1	jalapeño pepper, seeded and finely chopped	1
1 tbsp	canola oil	15 mL
2 1/2 tbsp	soy sauce	37 mL
1 1/2 tbsp	lime juice	22 mL
1 tsp	lime zest	5 mL
2 tbsp	brown sugar	30 mL
1 tsp	molasses	5 mL
1 tbsp	coconut cream	15 mL
1/2 cup	crunchy peanut butter	125 mL
1/4 cup	water	50 mL
1/4 tsp	cayenne	1 mL

🌀 Place the onion, garlic, ginger, pepper, oil, soy sauce, and lime juice in a blender or food processor. Blend until smooth, then transfer to a bowl.

🌀 Whisk in the remaining ingredients.

🌀 Makes 1 1/2 cups (375 mL)	per tablespoon (15 mL) calories 47.2 g fat 3.5 g fibre 0.4 **calorie breakdown** % protein 13 % fat 63 % carbohydrate 24

Ginger Lemon Salad Dressing

Every cook needs a salad dressing that can be thrown together from fresh ingredients. This one goes well with tossed greens and with fruit.

2 tbsp	lemon or lime juice	30 mL
1 tsp	lemon or lime zest	5 mL
1 tsp	white wine vinegar	5 mL
1 clove	garlic, finely chopped	1
1 1/2 tsp	grated ginger	7 mL
1 tsp	honey	5 mL
1/4 cup	olive oil	75 mL
salt and pepper to taste		

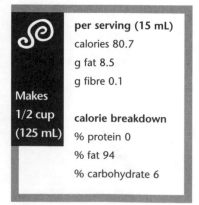 Mix lemon juice, lemon zest, vinegar, garlic, ginger, and honey. Whisk in oil. Add salt and pepper to taste. Toss with fresh greens.

Great & lite

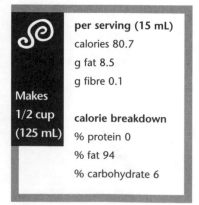 Makes 1/2 cup (125 mL)	per serving (15 mL)
	calories 80.7
	g fat 8.5
	g fibre 0.1
	calorie breakdown
	% protein 0
	% fat 94
	% carbohydrate 6

Ginger Pear Chutney

Adapted from Bruce Cost's *Ginger East to West*

This chutney is one of the best we have ever eaten. The hazard of trying this one, of course, is that all others will be compared with it and may be found wanting.

5 cups	pears cut into 1/2-inch (1.5 cm) cubes	1.25 L
1/2 cup	coarsely chopped ginger	125 mL
4 cloves	garlic, smashed	4
1 cup	chopped onion	250 mL
1 lb	brown sugar	550 mL
1 1/2 cups	cider vinegar	375 mL
1/2 cup	fresh lemon or lime juice	125 mL
5 to 10	fresh red chili peppers, seeded and diced	5 to 10
3	limes sliced or chopped very thin	3
peel of 2 large oranges, thinly sliced or cut into 1/2-inch (1.5 cm) cubes		
1/2 lb	raisins	375 mL
2 cups	diced fresh pineapple	500 mL
2	cinnamon sticks	2
2 tsp	nutmeg	10 mL
1/2 tsp	ground cloves	2 mL
2 tsp	salt or to taste	10 mL
1 tsp	white pepper	5 mL

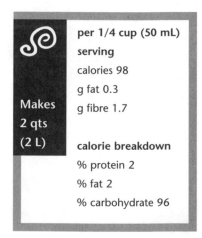 Put pears, ginger, garlic, onion, sugar, vinegar, and lemon juice in a large saucepan and simmer for 5 minutes.

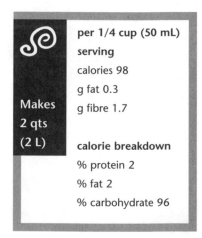 Add the rest of the ingredients and simmer for 20 to 30 minutes. Store in jars in the refrigerator for up to 6 months.

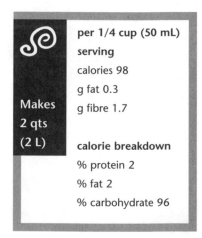 Makes 2 qts (2 L)	per 1/4 cup (50 mL) serving
	calories 98
	g fat 0.3
	g fibre 1.7
	calorie breakdown
	% protein 2
	% fat 2
	% carbohydrate 96

Fresh Ginger Chutney

Adapted from Time Life's *Foods of the World: Recipes: The Cooking of India*

A fabulous chutney that can be made in a jiffy, it goes well with everything from fishcakes to roast beef. We have even been known to throw it into a stir-fry for added flavour.

1 1/2 cups fresh lemon juice		375 mL
1 cup	coarsely chopped ginger	250 mL
1/2 cup	golden raisins	125 mL
2 tbsp	finely chopped garlic	30 mL
2 tsp	salt	10 mL

🌀 In an electric blender combine lemon juice, ginger, raisins, garlic, and salt and blend at high speed until the mixture is reduced to a smooth purée.

🌀 Serve the chutney at once or refrigerate until ready to use.

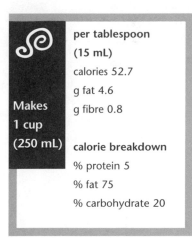

	per 1/8 cup (30 mL) serving
🌀	calories 37.3
	g fat 0.1
Makes 1 1/2 cups (375 mL)	g fibre 0.8
	calorie breakdown
	% protein 5
	% fat 2
	% carbohydrate 93

Fresh Coconut Chutney

Adapted from Time Life's *Foods of the World: Recipes: The Cooking of India*

This recipe proves beyond a doubt that fresh chutneys are as good as cooked ones. If you put this coconut chutney on the table people will eat it until it disappears, even if they have to scrape it out of the bowl with a spoon!

1 cup	coarsely peeled, chopped fresh coconut	250 mL
1/4 cup	fresh lemon juice	50 mL
1/2 cup	onion, finely chopped	125 mL
1/4 cup	ginger, finely chopped	125 mL
1	fresh hot chili	1
2 tsp	salt	10 mL
3 tbsp	canola oil	45 mL
1 tbsp	black mustard seeds	15 mL
1 tbsp	urad dal*	15 mL

🌀 Combine coconut and lemon juice in a blender or food processor and blend until the coconut is reduced to a smooth purée. Then add onion, ginger, chili, and salt and blend again.

🌀 In a heavy skillet, heat the canola oil over high heat until it begins to smoke. Drop in mustard seeds, fry for 10 seconds and add the urad dal, stirring constantly for 1 minute to coat evenly with oil. Then add the coconut mixture to the skillet and cook for 1 minute longer. Do not let the coconut brown. Serve immediately or chill in the refrigerator, where it can be kept for 2 or 3 days.

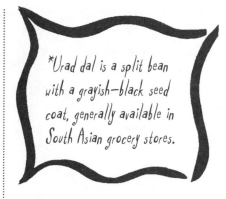

*Urad dal is a split bean with a grayish–black seed coat, generally available in South Asian grocery stores.

	per tablespoon (15 mL)
🌀	calories 52.7
	g fat 4.6
Makes 1 cup (250 mL)	g fibre 0.8
	calorie breakdown
	% protein 5
	% fat 75
	% carbohydrate 20

Ginger Rhubarb Chutney

Adapted from Carol Ferguson and Margaret Fraser,
A Century of Canadian Home Cooking: 1900 Through the '90s

Before the advent of fresh produce marketing, rhubarb was the first harvest in Nova Scotia, after dandelion greens, to break the monotony of the long winter diet of salted, dried, and canned foods. Rhubarb has recently become a fashionable ingredient in new age recipes, but nothing brings back the feeling of the "good old days" like rhubarb chutney.

6 cups	sliced rhubarb	1.5 L
5 cups	chopped peeled apples	1.25 L
4 cups	packed brown sugar	1 L
1 tsp	whole cloves	5 mL
1 tbsp	grated ginger or 1/4 cup (50 mL) minced preserved ginger	15 mL
1 clove	garlic	1 clove
1 cup	raisins	250 mL
1 tsp	salt	5 mL
1 tsp	cinnamon	5 mL
1 1/2 cups	vinegar	375 mL
1/2 cup	water	125 mL

In a heavy saucepan, combine rhubarb, apples, and sugar.

Tie cloves in a cheesecloth; add to fruit along with grated or minced ginger, garlic, raisins, salt, cinnamon, vinegar, and water. Bring to a boil, and boil gently, stirring often, until thickened, about 1 hour. Remove spice bag.

Pour into sterilized canning jars. Seal and process in boiling water bath for 10 minutes.

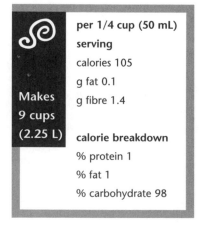

Makes 9 cups (2.25 L)

per 1/4 cup (50 mL) serving
calories 105
g fat 0.1
g fibre 1.4

calorie breakdown
% protein 1
% fat 1
% carbohydrate 98

Ginger Pineapple Salsa

Ginger gets lost in a hot salsa, but in delicate ones such as this pineapple salsa, it adds another dimension. A scoop of this salsa on lettuce or endive makes an exciting summer salad.

1 cup	ripe fresh pineapple, diced	250 mL
1/4 cup	finely chopped red pepper	50 mL
1 or 2	jalapeño peppers, cut in thin rings	1 or 2
2 tbsp	finely minced ginger	30 mL
1 tbsp	chopped cilantro	15 mL
1 tbsp	chopped mint	15 mL
1/4 cup	lime juice	50 mL

To the diced pineapple add the chopped red pepper, jalapeño peppers, ginger, cilantro, mint, and lime juice. Mix well.

Refrigerate for at least 1/2 hour before using.

Serves 4

per serving
calories 27.9
g fat 0.2
g fibre 0.8

calorie breakdown
% protein 5
% fat 7
% carbohydrate 89

Cranberry Ginger Relish

A variant of a recipe used by our mothers, this relish goes especially well with the Lean Turkey Loaf on page 68.

4 cups	cranberries	1 L
2	oranges, quartered	2
1/2 cup	honey	125 mL
1/4 cup	grated ginger	50 mL
1/3 cup	toasted walnuts (optional)	75 mL

In blender or food processor add cranberries, oranges, and honey and chop. The relish should be slightly chunky, not a purée. Fold toasted walnuts (if using) into the mixture and chill before serving.

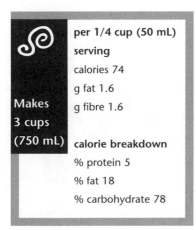

per 1/4 cup (50 mL)
serving
calories 74
g fat 1.6
g fibre 1.6

Makes
3 cups
(750 mL)

calorie breakdown
% protein 5
% fat 18
% carbohydrate 78

Ginger Rhubarb Conserve

This tangy exotic marmalade adds zing to toast, muffins, and tea biscuits.

6 cups	fresh rhubarb, cut into 1/2-inch (1 cm) pieces	1.5 L
3 cups	sugar	750 mL
1	orange	1
1/2	lemon	1/2
1/2 cup	water	125 mL
1/2 cup	ginger, coarsely chopped	125 mL
1 tsp	powdered ginger	5 mL
1 cup	golden raisins	250 mL
1/2 cup	walnuts, chopped	125 mL

In a large bowl layer rhubarb and sugar. Cover lightly and let stand overnight.

Slice orange and lemon thinly, discarding any seeds. Transfer citrus fruit to a large pot. Pour in water, cover and cook over a low heat for about 20 minutes, or until the rind is tender and translucent.

Add sugary rhubarb, ginger, and raisins, stirring well. Increase heat to high and bring to a full rapid boil. Adjust heat so the conserve bubbles briskly and cook for about 20 minutes, stirring frequently to prevent scorching. Add nuts and cook 5 minutes more, or until conserve thickens and sets.

Immediately pour into hot sterilized jars leaving 1/2-inch (1 cm) head space. Seal with wax.

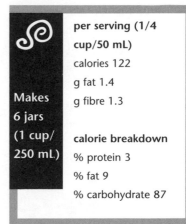

per serving (1/4 cup/50 mL)
calories 122
g fat 1.4
g fibre 1.3

Makes
6 jars
(1 cup/
250 mL)

calorie breakdown
% protein 3
% fat 9
% carbohydrate 87

Ginger Lemon Marmalade

*This marmalade packs a wallop and makes oat cakes
even more irresistible.*

3	large lemons	3
3 cups	cold water	750 mL
1 cup	ginger,	
	coarsely chopped	250 mL
1/4 cup	cold water	50 mL
4 cups	sugar	1L

🌀 Cut off lemon ends and cut lemons lengthwise into quarters and then cut crosswise into thin slices. Place in a bowl along with 3 cups (750 mL) of cold water. Cover bowl tightly and let stand for 24 hours at room temperature.

🌀 Transfer lemon slices with the soaking water to a large, heavy saucepan. Bring to a simmer over medium-high heat. Cover partially and adjust heat so that mixture barely simmers. Cook 45 minutes, stirring occasionally.

🌀 Meanwhile, purée chopped ginger with the 1/4 cup (50 mL) of cold water in a food processor or blender, stopping occasionally to scrape down the sides of the bowl. Strain mixture through a sieve, pressing down on the ginger solids with a spoon to extract as much juice as possible. Reserve the ginger juice.

🌀 Add sugar to lemon mixture and stir until dissolved. Add reserved ginger juice. Boil gently, uncovered, until the mixture thickens, about 1 hour.

🌀 Spoon preserves into hot sterilized jars to 1/4 inch (0.5 cm) from the top. Seal with wax.

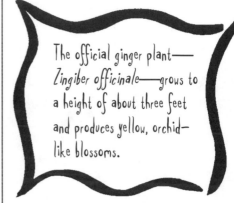

The official ginger plant—
Zingiber officinale—grows to
a height of about three feet
and produces yellow, orchid-
like blossoms.

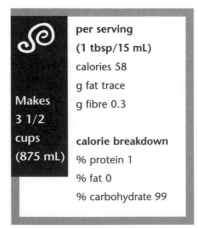

**Makes
3 1/2
cups
(875 mL)**

**per serving
(1 tbsp/15 mL)**
calories 58
g fat trace
g fibre 0.3

calorie breakdown
% protein 1
% fat 0
% carbohydrate 99

Pickled Ginger Appetizers

Pickled ginger, available in jars or plastic bags in specialty food stores, comes in its natural colour and dyed red. While we prefer the former, either one makes a tasty starter when combined with smoked fish, ham, fresh fruits, or cheese. (It also makes a statement in a meat sandwich or a green salad.) Although most people prefer to buy their ginger already pickled, it is easy to make and we think it tastes better from our own kitchens.

Pickled Ginger

1 lb	**fresh young ginger, sliced crosswise into paper-thin rounds**	**500 mL**
1 1/2 tbsp salt		**22 mL**
1 cup	**rice wine or white vinegar**	**250 mL**
3 tbsp	**sugar**	**45 mL**

☙ Arrange the ginger rounds in a single layer on a baking pan. Sprinkle with salt and cover tightly with plastic wrap. Let sit overnight at room temperature.

☙ Transfer to a large glass jar. Add the vinegar and sugar. Cover tightly and shake vigorously to combine the ingredients.

Refrigerate at least 1 week before serving. The ginger will keep up to 3 months if stored in the refrigerator.

Suggested Appetizers
Pickled ginger
Smoked mackerel
Smoked salmon
Smoked ham
Smoked chicken or turkey
Cheddar cheese
Cubed pears, cantaloupe, and pineapple cut into slivers or cubes, and tossed in lime or lemon juice to prevent discolouring
Greens
Crackers, wafers, or flat bread

☙ Arrange the ginger, smoked meats and fish, fruit and greens decoratively on a plate with crackers and let your guests put together mouth-watering combinations. Or make kebabs with pieces of pickled ginger, fruit, and smoked mackerel, chicken, salmon, or ham.

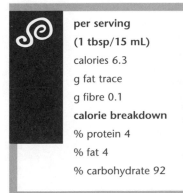

**per serving
(1 tbsp/15 mL)**
calories 6.3
g fat trace
g fibre 0.1
calorie breakdown
% protein 4
% fat 4
% carbohydrate 92

Gingered Zucchini Appetizers

Nova Scotians are especially careful in the summertime to lock their cars to prevent friends from loading them up with their surplus zucchini, which grows from the size of a pencil to that of a watermelon in the blink of an eye. If you catch the zucchini when it's very young, this recipe is good enough to open any car door.

2	small zucchini	2
1 tbsp	canola oil	15 mL
1 tbsp	grated ginger	15 mL
2	garlic cloves, grated	2
3 tbsp	grated parmesan cheese	45 mL

Slice zucchini into coins and toss in canola oil. Spread coins in a single layer in a glass baking dish and sprinkle with grated ginger, garlic, and parmesan cheese. Broil for 2 to 3 minutes, or until brown. Serve warm.

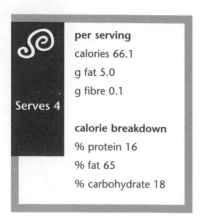

Serves 4

per serving
calories 66.1
g fat 5.0
g fibre 0.1

calorie breakdown
% protein 16
% fat 65
% carbohydrate 18

Smoked Salmon Ginger Butter Canapés

Willy Krauch's smoked salmon, a fine tradition in New York restaurants, comes from a small shop on the Eastern Shore of Nova Scotia. Although any smoked salmon will do in a pinch, the best always makes this recipe better. Because the flavour is so intense, a little bit goes a long way. It also freezes well, if, for some strange reason, you have any left over.

2 tbsp	minced ginger	30 mL
1 cup	unsalted butter, room temperature	250 mL
6 oz	thinly sliced smoked salmon or salmon bits	180 g
1 loaf	crusty Italian bread	1
freshly ground pepper		
1	lemon or lime	1

Place ginger and butter in a food processor. Process until smooth and fluffy. If using sliced salmon cut it up into bits. Mash bits of salmon into the ginger butter.

Cut bread into 16 slices. Toast lightly, cool, and cut each slice into three pieces.

Spread each piece of toasted bread with salmon ginger butter. Sprinkle with freshly ground pepper and a squeeze of lemon or lime juice.

Makes about 1 cup (250 mL) of butter, enough for 48 canapés

per serving
calories 68
g fat 4.3
g fibre 0.2

calorie breakdown
% protein 10
% fat 57
% carbohydrate 34

Prosciutto, Pear, and Chive Cornets with Ginger Cream

Make sure you have copies of this recipe at hand, because everyone will ask for it. To make the cornets easier to chew, ask your butcher to cut the prosciutto very thinly; even if it has holes, the prosciutto will wrap around the pear quite readily.

3 oz	cream cheese,	
	softened	75 g
2 tsp	grated ginger	10 mL
1 tsp	milk or cream	5 mL
1 tsp	English-style dry mustard	5 mL
pepper to taste		
2	firm ripe pears	2
juice of 1 lemon		
20	thin slices of prosciutto	
	(about 1/2 lb/250 g),	
	halved crosswise	20
40	fresh chives, cut in	
	3-inch (8 cm) lengths	40
or thinly sliced scallion pieces		

Use an electric mixer to beat together the cream cheese, ginger, milk or cream, mustard, and pepper until mixture is smooth.

Halve, core, and cut each pear lengthwise into 20 slices.

In a bowl toss the slices gently with lemon juice, coating them thoroughly.

Spread 1/4 teaspoon (1 mL) of the ginger cream on 1 piece of prosciutto, arrange 1 pear slice and 2 of the chive lengths or scallion bits in the centre, and fold the sides of the prosciutto to enclose the pear and chives or scallions in a bite-size cone shape. Continue to make cornets with the remaining ginger cream, prosciutto, pears, and chives or scallions in the same manner and arrange them decoratively on a platter. The cornets may be made 1 hour in advance and kept tightly covered and chilled.

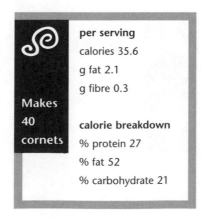

Makes 40 cornets

per serving
calories 35.6
g fat 2.1
g fibre 0.3

calorie breakdown
% protein 27
% fat 52
% carbohydrate 21

Camembert with Ginger Pear Chutney

Don't save this recipe for special occasions. It is easy to prepare and is melt-in-your-mouth delicious with Ginger Pear Chutney (see page 10) or Ginger Rhubarb Chutney (see page 12).

1	round of camembert	1
1 cup	Ginger Pear or Ginger	
	Rhubarb Chutney	250 mL

Place cheese on an ovenproof dish and pour chutney over the top.

Bake in preheated oven at 350°F (180°C) for 10 to 15 minutes, or until the cheese is hot and soft.

Serve with crackers or crusty bread.

Serves 4

per serving
calories 258
g fat 12.9
g fibre 2.0

calorie breakdown
% protein 16
% fat 43
% carbohydrate 40

Lemon Stuffed with Chickpea Pâté

Adapted from Yamuna Devi's *The Best of Lord Krishna's Cuisine*

Always pleasing to both the eye and the palate, this tasty dish makes a lovely small dinner party starter. We are indebted to Mary Filmore and Joanna Rankin for introducing us to The Best of Lord Krishna's Cuisine.

4	large lemons	4
1 1/2 inch	piece of ginger,	
	sliced	4 cm
1 or 2	jalapeño peppers	1 or 2
3 oz	cream cheese,	
	cut into small pieces	85 g
2 cups	drained, cooked chickpeas	
	(1 cup/100 g dry)	500 mL
3 tbsp	toasted sesame seeds	45 mL
6 tbsp	sour cream	90 mL
1/2 tsp	salt	2 mL
3 tbsp	olive oil	45 mL
1/2 tsp	yellow asafetida powder	
	(optional)*	2 mL
1/4 tsp	freshly ground	
	black pepper	1 mL
2 tsp	coarsely crushed dry-roasted	
	cumin seeds	10 mL
1 tbsp	minced fresh parsley	
	or chervil	15 mL
4	watercress sprigs	4

Bibb lettuce leaves
vegetable garnishes such as cucumber slices, tomato flowers, or radishes
crackers and/or vegetable crudités such as carrot sticks, broccoli florets, or celery

Cut off the tops of the lemons and reserve. Scoop out the pulp with a grapefruit spoon or sharp knife until the shells are empty. Squeeze the pulp through a strainer and save the juice. Trim a thin slice off the bottom of the lemons until they stand upright. Cover and chill until needed.

Fit a food processor with the metal blade. Turn on the motor, drop the ginger and jalapeño peppers through the feed tube and mince. Add the cream cheese and process until smooth. Drop in the chickpeas, sesame seeds, sour cream, salt, oil, asafetida (if using), and pepper.

per serving	
calories	440
g fat	29.7
g fibre	11.3

calorie breakdown
% protein 11
% fat 55
% carbohydrate 34

Serves 4

Process until smooth, adding up to 2 tablespoons (30 mL) of lemon juice for flavour and consistency. Add cumin seeds and pulse 2 or 3 times to crush them.

Fill the lemon cups with the pâté, piling it slightly over the edge of the cup. Sprinkle with parsley and top with the reserved caps. Place some Bibb lettuce and watercress on each plate and add vegetable garnishes. Chill until ready to serve.

Serve with crackers and/or vegetable crudités.

*Asafetida powder is used extensively in Indian cooking and serves as a digestive. If you cannot find it in a local grocery store, this recipe tastes just fine without it.

Breads
Breads
Breads
Breads
Breads
Breads
Breads
Breads

Ginger Walnut Tea Biscuits

This recipe never fails to please. It is easy to whip up just before the guests arrive so that the biscuits are piping hot and melt in your mouth.

2 cups	all-purpose flour	500 mL
4 tsp	baking powder	20 mL
1 tsp	salt	5 mL
1/2 cup	cold unsalted butter, cut into bits	125 mL
1/2 cup	grated ginger, including juice	125 mL
1/2 cup	brown sugar	125 mL
1 cup	finely chopped walnuts	250 mL
1/2 cup	milk	125 mL

Into a bowl sift together the flour, baking powder, and salt. Add butter, and blend the mixture until it resembles meal.

Stir in the grated ginger and juice, brown sugar, and walnuts. Add milk, and stir the mixture until it forms a soft sticky dough.

Drop the dough by rounded tablespoons onto an ungreased baking sheet and bake biscuits in the middle of preheated oven at 425°F (220°C) for 15 to 17 minutes, or until they are golden brown.

	per serving
	calories 177
	g fat 10
	g fibre 0.9
Makes 18 small biscuits	
	calorie breakdown
	% protein 8
	% fat 49
	% carbohydrate 43

Ginger Scones

At the restaurant associated with the Buderim Ginger Factory in Yandina, Australia, they add preserved ginger and dates to their scones. Served with Ginger Lemon Marmalade (see page 14) and clotted cream, these scones make a mouth-watering centrepiece to a cozy afternoon tea.

1 1/2 cups	all-purpose flour	375 mL
1/2 cup	whole wheat flour	125 mL
1 1/2 tbsp	baking powder	22 mL
1/2 tsp	salt	2 mL
4 tbsp	chilled butter	60 mL
1/2 cup	light cream	125 mL
1	egg, beaten	1
1/2 cup	chopped preserved ginger	125 mL
1/2 cup	chopped dates	125 mL
milk for brushing		

🍥 Combine flours. Add baking powder and salt to flours and sift into mixing bowl. Cut in the butter, add cream, egg, preserved ginger, and dates. Blend just enough to mix.

🍥 Turn onto a floured board. Knead lightly and roll 1/2-inch (1.5 cm) thick.

🍥 Cut into triangles or, using a floured cutter, 2-inch (5 cm) rounds. Brush with milk to make them shiny.

🍥 Place on an ungreased baking pan and bake in preheated oven at 450°F (230°C) for 12 to 15 minutes, or until done.

Variation: *Strawberry Ginger Shortcakes can be made by cutting warm scones in half, buttering the bottom half and then spooning crushed sugared strawberries over the buttered half of the scone, adding the top half, more crushed strawberries, and smothering the whole in whipped cream. Yum!*

🍥

per serving
calories 154
g fat 5.7
g fibre 1.8

Makes 12 scones

calorie breakdown
% protein 9
% fat 33
% carbohydrate 58

While it is known that ginger was first cultivated in the Far East, its origins have been lost in the mists of time. The Arabs are credited with planting ginger in East Africa, but when or how this process took place is unknown. The Arabs called the ginger that they sold in Europe *zinjabil*, from their word for Zanzibar, or Black Africa. It is from this word that the Latin term for the well-travelled little rhizome *Zingiber officinale* is derived.

Lardy Bread

This traditional British fruit-filled bread is tasty, nutritious, and keeps well. Usually served for breakfast or afternoon tea, it is scrumptious with coffee. We have maintained the proportion of lard to flour but increased the amount of ginger usually found in lardy bread recipes.

Bread

1 1/4 cups	warm water	300 mL
1 tbsp	sugar	15 mL
1/2 tbsp	dry yeast	7 mL
4 cups	all-purpose flour	1L
1 tsp	salt	5 mL
1 tsp	canola oil	5 mL
1/2 cup	lard, cut in small pieces	125 mL
1/4 cup	sugar	50 mL
1/2 tsp	grated nutmeg	2 mL
1/2 tsp	cinnamon	2 mL
1 tsp	ground ginger	5 mL
1 cup	currants	250 mL
1 cup	chopped preserved ginger	250 mL

Glaze

3 tbsp	sugar	45 mL
3 tbsp	water	45 mL

Stir 1 tbsp (15 mL) sugar into 1/4 cup (50 mL) of warm water. Sprinkle yeast over the top of the water. Keep warm until the yeast becomes puffy and frothy, 15 to 20 minutes.

Measure half the flour in a large bowl. Add the salt, the rest of the warm water, activated yeast, and canola oil. Beat until the dough is stretchy and sticky.

Add enough of the remaining flour to make a stiff dough. Knead on a floured surface until smooth.

Wash and lightly grease the large bowl. Return the dough to the bowl, cover, and leave to rise in a warm place for 1 to 1 1/2 hours, or until double the bulk.

In the meantime, mix 1/4 cup (50 mL) sugar with grated nutmeg, cinnamon, ground ginger, currants, and preserved ginger. Set aside.

Knead dough lightly, then roll it out into a 1/4-inch (1 cm) thick oblong shape, that is, three times as long as it is wide. Sprinkle the upper two-thirds of the oblong with half the lard and half the currant mixture. Fold the uncovered third up and then fold again. Lightly press the open ends with your fingers, and then roll out again into an oblong. Repeat the process with the remaining lard and currant mixture.

Roll out and shape the dough to fit an 8-inch (20 cm) round pan. (You may wish to use a spring-form pan but watch the bread carefully during the baking process because the lard may leak out and wreak havoc in your oven.) Put the dough in the pan, cover, and leave to rise in a warm place for 1 hour or until almost doubled in bulk.

Bake in a preheated oven at 375°F (190°C) for 35 minutes. Mix the glaze ingredients and brush over the bread. Continue baking for 10 minutes or until golden brown. Allow to cool on a wire rack before serving.

Note: *The sealed edges will not completely hold during baking, but this contributes to the look of the bread.*

Makes 25 slices	per serving
	calories 176
	g fat 4.8
	g fibre 1.1
	calorie breakdown
	% protein 6
	% fat 25
	% carbohydrate 70

Ginger Cheese Muffins
Adapted from *Kate Aitken's Cookbook*

In the 1950s and 1960s, Kate Aitken's Cook Book *was a culinary staple in many Canadian kitchens. Cheese and ginger make a potent combination in this recipe.*

2 cups	all-purpose flour	500 mL
3 tsp	baking powder	15 mL
1/4 tsp	baking soda	1 mL
1/2 tsp	salt	2 mL
1/2 tsp	powdered ginger	2 mL
1	egg	1
2/3 cup	milk	150 mL
1/2 cup	corn syrup or	
	molasses	125 mL
1/4 cup	finely chopped	
	preserved ginger	50 mL
1/4 cup	melted shortening	
	or butter	50 mL
2/3 cup	grated	
	cheddar cheese	150 mL

Sift together dry ingredients. Grate the cheese. Set aside.

In a large bowl, beat egg until light. Add milk, syrup or molasses, and chopped ginger. Combine the two mixtures stirring as little as possible. (The batter will be stiff.)

Add the melted shortening or butter and cheese. Blend.

Fill 16 greased muffin tins 2/3 full. Bake in preheated oven at 350°F (180°C) until firm, about 20 minutes. Remove from oven, cover with a towel and let stand for 5 minutes before removing from pan. Serve hot.

per muffin
calories 135
g fat 3.7
g fibre 0.5

Makes 16 muffins

calorie breakdown
% protein 8
% fat 25
% carbohydrate 67

Another way of storing extra ginger is to place peeled coins of ginger in a glass jar and cover with vodka. Ginger slices keep indefinitely this way and the vodka takes on a new interest as well.

Ginger Lemon Muffins

These muffins—suggested by Hilary Taylor, who appreciates the value of ginger—make breakfast worth looking forward to, or have them as a satisfying snack any time of day.

1/2 cup	finely chopped ginger	125 mL
1/4 cup	sugar	50 mL
zest from	2 lemons	
2 cup	all-purpose flour	500 mL
1/2 tsp	salt	2 mL
2/3 tsp	baking soda	4 mL
2	eggs	2
1 cup	buttermilk	250 mL
1/4 cup	butter, melted	50 mL

🌀 Combine the ginger and sugar in a small dish and heat in microwave at high for 1 minute. Stir in the lemon zest.

🌀 Sift together flour, salt, and baking soda. Stir in the ginger and lemon mixture.

🌀 Beat the egg until light. Add the buttermilk and melted butter. Combine with the flour mixture, stirring as little as possible.

🌀 Fill 16 buttered muffin tins three-quarters full with the batter. Bake in preheated oven at 375°F (190°C) for 15 or 20 minutes. Serve warm to get the full advantage of the butter.

🌀 **Makes 16 muffins**

per serving
calories 133
g fat 4.0
g fibre 0.6

calorie breakdown
% protein 8
% fat 23
% carbohydrate 69

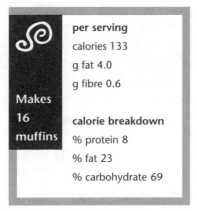

Blueberry Ginger Nut Loaf

Heather's recipe makes a delicious sweetbread for leisurely afternoon teas or late summer picnics.

2	eggs	2
1 cup	sugar	250 mL
1 cup	milk or milk mixed with juice of 1 orange	250 mL
3 tbsp	canola oil	45 mL
zest of 1 orange		
2 cups	all-purpose flour	500 mL
1 cup	whole wheat flour	250 mL
4 tsp	baking powder	20 mL
1 tsp	salt	2 mL
1 cup	blueberries	250 mL
1/2 cup	chopped walnuts	125 mL
1/2 cup	grated ginger	125 mL

🌀 Beat eggs and add sugar, mixing thoroughly. Add milk, oil, and orange zest. Sift together flours, baking powder, and salt, and add to the liquid mixture. Stir only until blended. Fold in blueberries, walnuts, and ginger.

🌀 Pour into 2 greased 9 x 5 inch (12 x 22 cm) loaf pans and bake at 350°F (180°C) for 1 hour, or until it tests done with a toothpick.

🌀 **Makes 2 loaves, 32 slices**

per slice
calories 108
g fat 3.2
g fibre 1.2

calorie breakdown
% protein 9
% fat 26
% carbohydrate 65

Fruit Gazpacho

Adapted from Sal Gilbertie's *Kitchen Herbs*

This marvellous soup should be made in the summer when cantaloupes, cucumbers, and tomatoes are juicy and flavourful—the freshness of the ingredients really makes a difference in this much-admired starter. If locally available oranges are not worthy of juicing, use a high-grade frozen orange juice.

3	medium tomatoes, peeled, seeded, and finely chopped	3
1	cantaloupe, peeled, seeded, and finely chopped	1
1	cucumber, peeled and chopped	1
1	large white onion, chopped	1
1	sweet yellow pepper, chopped	1
1	sweet red pepper, chopped	1
1	clove garlic, minced	1
1	jalapeño pepper, minced	1
2 tbsp	minced ginger	30 mL
1/4 cup	chopped fresh coriander	50 mL
zest of 1 orange		
zest of 1 lime		
1 1/2 cups orange juice (fresh or frozen)		375 mL
3 tbsp	fresh lime juice	45 mL
salt and pepper to taste		
sprigs of coriander for garnish		

 In a food processor or by hand finely mince together tomatoes, cantaloupe, cucumber, onion, yellow pepper, red pepper, garlic, jalapeño pepper, ginger, and coriander. (If using a food processor, be careful not to turn the ingredients into juice.)

 Put the minced vegetables and herbs in a large bowl, add orange and lime zests, and stir in orange and lime juices. Season to taste with salt and pepper.

 Chill for at least 1 hour.

 Ladle into chilled soup bowls and garnish with sprigs of fresh coriander.

Serves 4

per serving
calories 151
g fat 1.1
g fibre 5.5

calorie breakdown
% protein 10
% fat 6
% carbohydrate 84

Lemon Ginger Broth

This soup has surprisingly soothing powers for curing whatever ails you. Ginger adds spunk to an otherwise plain broth.

6 cups	chicken broth	1.5 L
2 tbsp	grated ginger	30 mL
salt to taste		
freshly ground pepper to taste		
1 tsp	cumin seeds, roasted and ground	5 mL
zest and juice of 1 lemon		
coriander or parsley leaves for garnish		

🌀 In a saucepan bring broth and ginger to a boil. Simmer for 30 minutes, or until broth is reduced to about half.

🌀 Add salt, pepper, cumin, and lemon zest. Simmer for 2 minutes and add lemon juice.

🌀 Garnish with coriander or parsley leaves and serve.

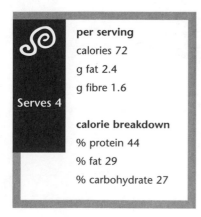

🌀	**per serving**
	calories 72
	g fat 2.4
	g fibre 1.6
Serves 4	
	calorie breakdown
	% protein 44
	% fat 29
	% carbohydrate 27

Gingered Carrot and Orange Soup

This is Margaret's version of one of the great tastes of the twentieth century. Variations have been suggested by Leslie Maitland, Jill Smillie, and Mary Ganong, proof-positive that carrot soup ranks among the most popular of soups. And it's healthy, too!

2 tbsp	butter	30 mL
4 cups	thinly sliced carrots	1 L
1	large onion, chopped	1
3 tbsp	grated ginger	45 mL
3 cups	chicken or vegetable stock	750 mL
1 cup	orange juice (fresh or frozen)	250 mL
salt and pepper to taste		
1/4 cup	whipping cream	75 mL
orange zest for garnish		
sprigs of parsley or cilantro for garnish		

Variations: *Try substituting squash, pumpkins, or parsnips for carrots or using 2 cups (500 mL) of carrots and 2 cups (500 mL) of apples, or adding a teaspoon of curry or cumin powder. Serve with a dollop of yogurt or sour cream.*

🌀 In a saucepan over low heat, melt butter. Stir in carrots, onion, and ginger. Cover and cook 5 minutes. Pour in chicken or vegetable stock and bring to a boil. Reduce heat and simmer, covered, for about 15 minutes, or until carrots are tender.

🌀 Remove from the heat and cool slightly. In a food processor or blender, purée carrot mixture until smooth.

🌀 Pour purée back into saucepan and stir in orange juice. Add salt and pepper to taste, stir in whipping cream, and gently reheat—do not boil. Garnish with orange zest and sprigs of parsley or cilantro.

🌀	**per serving**
	calories 267
	g fat 10.7
	g fibre 7.1
Serves 4	
	calorie breakdown
	% protein 11
	% fat 35
	% carbohydrate 54

Ginger and Sweet Potato Soup

Nutritious, low-calorie, easy to make, and teeming with flavour. What more could you ask?

6 cups	sweet potatoes, cubed	1.5 L
3 1/2 cups	chicken or soy stock	875 mL
1 tbsp	ginger, minced	15 mL
1/2 cup	unsweetened coconut milk	125 mL
3 tbsp	lime juice	45 mL
salt and pepper to taste		
1/4 cup	sliced toasted almonds	50 mL
1/4 cup	fresh coriander	50 mL
1 tsp	lime zest	5 mL

In a saucepan, combine sweet potatoes, chicken or soy stock, and ginger. Bring to a boil. Reduce heat, cover, and simmer for about 10 minutes, or until the potatoes are tender.

Transfer to a blender or food processor and purée until mixture is smooth. Return mixture to saucepan. Whisk in coconut milk, lime juice, and salt and pepper to taste. Cook over low heat just until heated through.

Ladle into individual bowls; sprinkle with toasted almonds, coriander, and lime zest. Serve immediately.

Parsnip, Lemon, and Ginger Soup

Adapted from Claire Macdonald of Macdonald's *Celebrations*

Parsnips are a favourite root vegetable in the Maritimes partly because they are hardy and will survive in the ground over winter. They have a distinctive flavour that ginger complements nicely. This soup freezes well if you need a tasty make-ahead starter.

4 tbsp	butter or vegetable oil	60 mL
2	medium onions, skinned and chopped	2
4	good-size parsnips, peeled and chopped	4
zest and juice of 1/2 lemon		
3 tbsp	ginger, peeled and chopped	45 mL
4 cups	chicken stock	1 L
salt and freshly ground black pepper to taste		
2 tbsp	finely chopped parsley	30 mL

Melt butter or oil in a large saucepan, and add the chopped onions. Cook for 5 minutes, stirring occasionally.

Add the chopped parsnips, lemon zest, and ginger. Cook for a further 5 minutes, then pour on the stock. With the saucepan half-covered with a lid, simmer gently until the parsnips are soft.

Cool the soup slightly before puréeing in a food processor. Season with lemon juice, salt, and pepper to taste.

Reheat, and just before serving stir in the chopped parsley.

per serving
calories 262
g fat 6.6
g fibre 5.7

calorie breakdown
% protein 10
% fat 22
% carbohydrate 68

Serves 8

per serving
calories 123
g fat 6.8
g fibre 0.8

calorie breakdown
% protein 12
% fat 48
% carbohydrate 41

Serves 8

Gingered Corn Chowder with Coriander

This versatile soup goes over well in summer or winter, for lunch or dinner, with fresh, frozen, or canned corn. We keep this one on hand in the freezer, just in case we need a quick, hearty starter.

3	strips bacon	3
1	onion, chopped	1
1/2 tsp	dried thyme	2 mL
1/2 tsp	dried crumbled marjoram	2 mL
1/4 tsp	mace	1 mL
1/4 tsp	black pepper	1 mL
2 tbsp	finely chopped ginger	30 mL
1/2	sweet red pepper, finely chopped	1/2
1/2	sweet green pepper, finely chopped	1/2
3 cups	corn kernels (fresh or frozen), chopped in a food processor for 15 seconds	750 mL
	or	
	3 cups (750 mL) good quality cream-style corn	
3 1/2 cups chicken stock		875 mL
1 cup	heavy cream	250 mL
salt to taste		
1/3 cup coriander		75 mL

In a heavy saucepan, cook the bacon over low heat, stirring until all the fat is rendered. Transfer the bacon with a slotted spoon to paper towels to drain.

Add to the pan the onion, thyme, marjoram, mace, and black pepper. Cook the mixture over moderate heat, stirring for 3 to 4 minutes, or until the onion is browned lightly. Add the ginger and peppers, and cook the mixture, stirring occasionally, for 5 minutes.

Add the corn and the stock, bring the liquid to a boil, and simmer the mixture, covered, stirring occasionally, for 30 minutes. Add cream and salt to taste, bring the soup just to a simmer, and stir in coriander.

Serve the soup sprinkled with the crumbled cooked bacon.

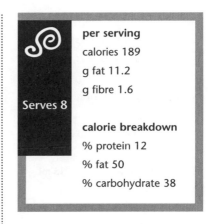

Serves 8

per serving
calories 189
g fat 11.2
g fibre 1.6

calorie breakdown
% protein 12
% fat 50
% carbohydrate 38

Thai Soup with Chicken and Ginger

This is a quick and easy version of a classic Thai soup. Like all traditional chicken soups, it offers comfort and nutrition as well as good taste. This recipe is best using fresh young ginger, which is less fibrous than mature ginger.

1/2 lb	boneless chicken breast meat	250 g
1 tbsp	lemon zest	15 mL
2 tbsp	ginger, cut into thin slivers	30 mL
1	chili pepper, finely chopped	1
1	can coconut milk (398 mL)	1
1 cup	water or chicken stock	250 mL
2 tbsp	lemon juice	30 mL
1 tbsp	lime juice	15 mL
1 tbsp	fish sauce	15 mL
1/4 tsp	sugar	1 mL
fresh coriander leaves		

Slice chicken into thin strips (1/4 inch/5 mm).

In a small bowl, mix together lemon zest, ginger, and chilies. Set aside.

Heat coconut milk and water or chicken stock in a saucepan for 2 to 3 minutes, but do not let the mixture boil. Add the reserved lemon zest, ginger and chili mixture. Simmer for another 2 minutes, stirring constantly. Add the chicken strips and simmer over medium heat for another 5 minutes. It is important that the chicken be done but not overcooked.

Add lemon juice, lime juice, fish sauce, and sugar. Stir for another 1 to 2 minutes.

Serve immediately, garnished with chopped coriander leaves.

Variations: Substitute seafood (shrimp, lobster, and scallops) for chicken. For a festive "look," add 1/2 cup (125 mL) of finely chopped red pepper.

Serves 6

per serving
calories 175
g fat 14
fibre 0.3

calorie breakdown
% protein 23
% fat 69
% carbohydrate 8

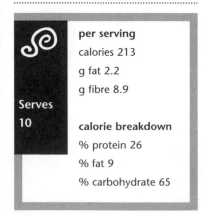

Serves 10

per serving
calories 213
g fat 2.2
g fibre 8.9

calorie breakdown
% protein 26
% fat 9
% carbohydrate 65

Lentil and Barley Soup

One of Heather's creations, this soup is a hit with our friends, especially with corn bread on the side.

8 cups	chicken stock	2 L
2 cups	lentils	500 mL
1/2 cup	pearl barley	125 mL
1 tsp	toasted sesame oil	5 mL
2 tsp	canola oil	10 mL
4	large cloves of garlic, minced	4
3 tbsp	grated ginger	45 mL
1 cup	finely chopped celery	250 mL
1/2 cup	fresh parsley	125 mL
2 cups	onions chopped	500 mL
1/3 cup	soy sauce	75 mL
2 tbsp	lemon juice	30 mL
1/4 tsp	cayenne	1 mL

In a heavy pot, bring the stock to a boil. Stir in the lentils and barley, and simmer for about 30 minutes.

Meanwhile, in a large skillet, heat the oils, add the garlic, grated ginger, celery, parsley, and onion. Sauté until the vegetables are softened.

Add the vegetables to the cooked lentils and barley. Add the soy sauce, lemon juice, and cayenne. Simmer for 5 minutes and serve.

Spicy Corn and Tomato Soup

Adapted from *Jane Brody's Good Food Gourmet*

Even when we substituted canned tomatoes and corn for the fresh varieties, this marvellous cold soup still provoked raves.

Saffron Cream

3/4 tsp	butter	4 mL
3/4 tsp	minced garlic	4 mL
2 tsp	minced ginger	10 mL
1/8 tsp	saffron threads, crumbled & dissolved in 2 tbsp (30 mL) of warm water	0.5 mL
pinch of salt (optional)		
3/4 cup	plain yogurt	175 mL

Soup

2 tsp	whole cumin seeds, toasted	10 mL
1/3 cup	water	75 mL
2 tbsp	minced garlic	30 mL
2 tbsp	minced ginger	30 mL
1/2 tsp	turmeric	2 mL
1/2 tsp	allspice	2 mL
1/4 tsp	red pepper flakes	1 mL
1 tbsp	butter	15 mL
2 cups	onion, peeled and chopped	500 mL
6 cups	chicken or soy stock broth	1.5 L
3 1/2 lb	very ripe tomatoes or a 19 oz (540 mL) can of tomatoes	1.75 kg
freshly ground black pepper		
salt to taste (optional)		
2 cups	corn kernels (fresh, frozen, or canned) steamed for 2 minutes	500 mL
5	Anaheim chilies, roasted, peeled, seeded, and diced for garnish (optional)	5

🌀 Prepare the saffron cream by melting butter in a heavy saucepan over medium-low heat. Add the garlic and ginger to the pan and sauté for about a minute. Stir in the saffron in water and simmer for 1 more minute. Add a pinch of salt if using and remove pan from the heat. Stir in the yogurt and store in the refrigerator for at least 6 hours.

🌀 To prepare soup, grind the toasted cumin seeds in a blender. Add water, garlic, ginger, turmeric, allspice, and pepper flakes and purée the mixture. Set aside.

🌀 In a large, heavy saucepan over low heat, melt the butter. Sauté onions, stirring occasionally, for about 15 minutes, or until they are very soft.

🌀 Add the reserved spice mixture. Raise the heat to medium-low, and cook the ingredients, stirring often, for about 5 minutes, or until the liquid evaporates. Add broth and simmer the mixture for 50 minutes, or until the mixture is reduced by one-third.

🌀 Add tomatoes to the mixture, and purée the mixture in 3 or 4 batches in a blender or food processor. Then pass the mixture through a sieve or food mill to remove tomato skins and seeds.

🌀 Season soup with pepper and salt (optional) to taste, and refrigerate for at least 6 hours.

🌀 Before serving time, mix the steamed corn kernels into the soup, and let the soup stand at room temperature for about 20 minutes.

🌀 Garnish each portion with a swirl of chilled saffron cream and a sprinkling of the chilies.

Variation: This soup also makes an excellent base for a nippy seafood chowder. Simply add scallops, shrimp, crab meat, and lobster meat (in whatever proportions your taste and pocketbook allow) to the prepared soup, as well as 1/4 cup (50 mL) of medium-dry sherry, and simmer for 5 minutes, or until the seafood is just done. Top with a dollop of saffron cream and serve immediately.

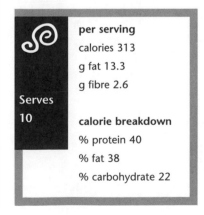

	per serving
🌀	calories 313
	g fat 13.3
	g fibre 2.6
Serves 10	
	calorie breakdown
	% protein 40
	% fat 38
	% carbohydrate 22

Yellow Split Pea Soup with Spiced Yogurt

Adapted from Deborah Madison with Edward Espe Brown's
The Greens Cookbook

After eating this soup you will feel so healthy and contented, you will want another helping for good measure. Make a big batch while you're at it so you can freeze some for a rainy day. We are grateful to Carroll Klein for bringing this fabulous recipe to our attention.

1 2/3 cups pre-soaked yellow
            split peas   400 mL
2 tbsp clarified butter   30 mL
1   large yellow onion, diced 1
2   cloves garlic,
        finely chopped   2
1 tbsp ginger, peeled and minced
        or more to taste   15 mL
1   bay leaf   1
1 tsp   salt   5 mL
1/2 tsp ground cumin   2 mL
1 tsp   ground cloves   5 mL
1   celery heart or two
        outer stalks, diced   1
2   medium carrots, peeled and
        cut into small squares 2
7 cups vegetable or
        chicken stock   1.75 L
grated zest and juice of 1 lemon
spiced yogurt (see below)
cilantro or parsley, chopped for
garnish

Soak the peas for 2 or more hours in enough cold water to cover them—about 3 times the amount of water to peas.

Warm the clarified butter in a soup pot and add the onion, garlic, ginger, bay leaf, salt, cumin, and cloves. Cook over medium heat for 3 to 4 minutes, stirring occasionally.

Drain the peas, and add them to the onion mixture along with celery, carrots, and vegetable or chicken stock. Bring to a boil and simmer until peas have completely fallen apart, about an hour.

Purée the soup in a blender and return to heat, adding more stock if necessary to achieve the desired consistency. Season to taste with additional salt, lemon zest, and lemon juice.

Serve the soup in warm bowls with a spoonful of spiced yogurt and a sprinkling of cilantro or parsley.

Spiced Yogurt

1/2 cup plain yogurt   125 mL
1/2 tsp turmeric   2 mL
1/2 tsp paprika   2 mL
1/4 tsp cayenne or more
        to taste   1 mL
1/4 tsp ground cumin seed   1 mL
pinch of salt

Whisk the yogurt until it is smooth; then stir in remaining ingredients.

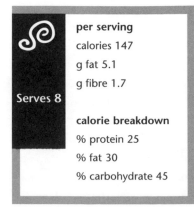

Serves 8

per serving
calories 147
g fat 5.1
g fibre 1.7

calorie breakdown
% protein 25
% fat 30
% carbohydrate 45

Dried Cod, Pork, and Ginger Soup

Adapted from Junko Lampert's *The Tofu Cookbook*

This recipe, recommended to us by Barbara LeBlanc, calls for fresh bacon, sometimes called pork belly. We added green onions for colour and recommend increasing the amount of ginger suggested below— after all, one can never have enough ginger!

7 oz	salted cod, dried	200 g
1/3 lb	fresh bacon	150 g
1/2 lb	tofu	225 g
2 tbsp	grated ginger or more to taste	30 mL
2	green onions	2
5 cups	soup stock	1.25 L
2 tbsp	sake	30 mL
1 tbsp	sesame oil	15 mL

Soak cod in cold water for 2 hours. Cut into bite-size pieces. Reserve the salty soaking water.

Cut sliced bacon into 1-inch (2.5 cm) pieces, fry slowly until crisp. Set aside.

Dice tofu into 1-inch (2.5 cm) cubes.

Peel ginger and shred into very thin threads.

Wash and chop green onions, including green stems.

Combine soup stock with 1 cup (250 mL) of the salty soaking water. (Those wishing to keep their salt intake to a minimum may wish to use less soaking water, but it does enhance the flavour of the soup.) Add cod and bacon and bring mixture to a boil. Lower heat and simmer for 1/2 hour. Skim off any fat that rises to the surface.

Add sake and tofu and simmer until the tofu rises to the surface.

Just before serving stir in ginger and green onions. Sprinkle with sesame oil. Ladle into heated soup bowls and serve.

per serving
calories 204
g fat 8.7
g fibre 0.1

Serves 8

calorie breakdown
% protein 55
% fat 39
% carbohydrate 5

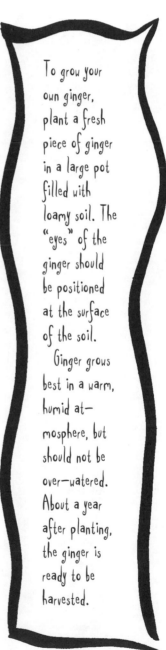

To grow your own ginger, plant a fresh piece of ginger in a large pot filled with loamy soil. The "eyes" of the ginger should be positioned at the surface of the soil.

Ginger grows best in a warm, humid atmosphere, but should not be over-watered. About a year after planting, the ginger is ready to be harvested.

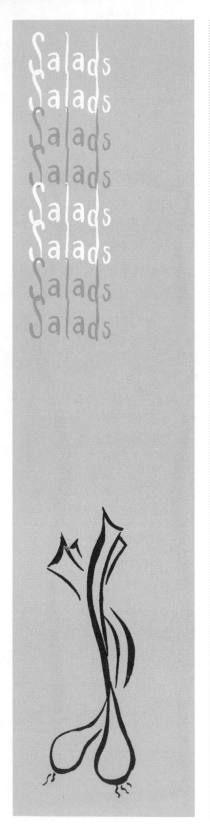

Chickpea and Ginger Salad

Adapted from Yamuna Devi's *The Best of Lord Krishna's Cuisine*

Serve this as a "salad chutney" or have it with seasonal fresh fruit for a light breakfast. If you are in a hurry, substitute canned chickpeas for the dried variety.

1/3 cup	whole chickpeas, sorted and soaked in 1 1/2 cups (360 mL) water overnight	50 g
1 1/2 inch piece of ginger		15 mL
1 1/2 tbsp fresh lime or lemon juice		22 mL
1/2 tsp	chat masala* (optional)	2 mL
1/4 tsp	freshly ground black pepper	1 mL

✏ Drain the chickpeas. Note that they are not cooked. Served this way they are pleasantly crunchy and digestible.

✏ Peel the ginger and slice into paper-thin rounds, then julienne in very thin strips.

✏ Combine all the ingredients in a small bowl, toss well, and serve.

per serving
calories 24
g fat 0.4
g fibre 0.9

Serves 4

calorie breakdown
% protein 19
% fat 12
% carbohydrate 68

*Chat masala is a spicy condiment that includes a variety of ingredients such as salt, pepper, cumin, coriander, ground ginger, nutmeg, cloves, mint leaf, tamarind, pomegranate seeds, dry mango, and perhaps other esoteric items such as bishops weeds, asafetida, and kachri.

Ginger, Grapefruit, and Avocado Salad

Heather's beautiful summer salad, when served on a large platter that enhances the shape of the whole lettuce leaves, is a pleasure to behold. Grapefruit, avocado, and ginger are sensational together.

Salad

1	head Butter lettuce	1
1	avocado, sliced	1
1	grapefruit, sectioned, membrane removed	1
2 tsp	chopped chives or green onions	10 mL

per serving
calories 226
g fat 20.5
g fibre 2.8

Serves 4

calorie breakdown
% protein 4
% fat 77
% carbohydrate 19

Dressing

3 tbsp	canola oil	45 mL
2 tsp	toasted sesame seed oil	10 mL
1 tbsp	soy sauce	15 mL
1	large garlic clove, crushed	1
1/4 cup	lemon juice	50 mL
2 tbsp	grated young ginger and juice	30 mL

🌀 Combine all ingredients for dressing.

🌀 Gently, wash and dry uncut lettuce leaves and place on a large platter.

🌀 Carefully add half the dressing to grapefruit and avocado sections in a bowl, toss lightly; then arrange on lettuce.

🌀 Drizzle the remaining dressing over entire salad and sprinkle with chopped chives. Serve on its own or with a light bread.

per serving
calories 350
g fat 15.1
g fibre 1.4

Serves 4

calorie breakdown
% protein 11
% fat 39
% carbohydrate 50

Ginger Couscous

Couscous is the easiest of all grains to prepare, which can only boost its appeal. Served cold as a salad or hot as an accompaniment to a main course, it makes a delectable dish.

3 tbsp	vegetable oil	45 mL
2	finely chopped onions	2
2 tbsp	ginger, minced	30 mL
2	garlic cloves, minced	2
1 cup	couscous	250 mL
1 cup	chicken stock	250 mL
1/2 tsp	toasted sesame oil or to taste	2 mL
3 tbsp	chopped, salted, dry-roasted peanuts or mixed toasted sunflower and sesame seeds	45 mL

🌀 In a large skillet, heat vegetable oil over moderately high heat until it is hot but not smoking, and in it sauté the onions, ginger, and garlic, stirring frequently, for 2 or 3 minutes.

🌀 Bring stock to boil. Add couscous, cover, remove from heat, and let stand for 5 minutes. Add ginger mixture and toasted sesame oil and stir in peanuts or mixed sunflower and sesame seeds.

Oriental Tuna Salad

Adapted from *Weight Watchers Healthy Life-Style Cookbook*

Transform canned tuna into a gourmet delight with this easy recipe.

1 (6-oz)	can flaked tuna	170 g
1/3 cup	finely chopped green onion	60 mL
1/3 cup	celery	60 mL
1/3 cup	bean sprouts	60 mL
3 tbsp	mayonnaise	45 mL
1 tbsp	soy sauce	15 mL
1 tbsp	grated ginger	15 mL
2	small cloves garlic, minced	2

🌀 Combine all ingredients in a bowl, mixing well.

🌀 Serve on bed of lettuce, as stuffing for tomatoes or green peppers, or make a fabulous sandwich on the bread of your choice.

per serving
calories 125
g fat 8.6
g fibre 0.3

Serves 4

calorie breakdown
% protein 30
% fat 63
% carbohydrate 7

Chinese Chicken Salad with Sesame Ginger Dressing

Adapted from *Just the Best: Favourite Recipes from Canada's Top Food Writers.*

This recipe, Lucy Waverman's contribution to the Women's Legal Education and Action Fund's fine cookbook Just the Best, *can cast summer hues over a winter's day.*

Salad

2 cups	spinach, washed and dried	500 mL
1	small Boston lettuce, washed and dried	1
2	green onions, slivered	2
1 cup	watercress leaves	250 mL
4	chicken breasts, grilled	4

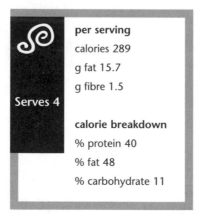

per serving
calories 289
g fat 15.7
g fibre 1.5

Serves 4

calorie breakdown
% protein 40
% fat 48
% carbohydrate 11

Dressing

4 tsp	soy sauce	20 mL
1/4 cup	vegetable oil	50 mL
1/2 cup	lime juice	125 mL
2 tsp	brown sugar	10 mL
2 tsp	sesame oil	10 mL
2 tsp	finely chopped ginger	10 mL
2 tsp	Dijon mustard	10 mL

🌀 Combine spinach, lettuce, green onions, and watercress leaves. Place on a platter and arrange warm chicken breasts on top.

🌀 In a small bowl whisk together the dressing ingredients and drizzle over salad.

Korean Vegetable Salad

This recipe works best when we take the time to do each vegetable separately to retain individual flavours.

Salad

1	small turnip, peeled and cut into strips	1
pinch of salt		
4 tbsp	olive oil	60 mL
1	small onion, finely chopped	1
1 cup	sliced mushrooms	250 mL
2	celery stalks, thinly sliced	2
3	green onions, chopped	3
1	carrot, cut into strips	1
1 tbsp	pine nuts or sesame seeds, toasted	15 mL

Dressing

3 tbsp	soy sauce	45 mL
1 tbsp	brown sugar	15 mL
1 tbsp	vinegar	15 mL
2 tbsp	grated ginger	30 mL
1/4 tsp	black pepper	1 mL

🌀 Sprinkle the turnip strips with salt and leave for 15 minutes.

🌀 Heat 2 tbsp (30 mL) of the oil in a frying pan. Add the turnip strips and fry until crisp. Drain on paper towels and leave to cool.

🌀 Add the chopped onion to the pan and fry until golden brown. Drain on paper and leave to cool.

🌀 Add the mushrooms to the pan and fry until tender, adding the remaining oil if necessary. Drain on paper towels and leave to cool.

🌀 Fry the celery until golden, then drain on paper towels and leave to cool.

🌀 Mix all the ingredients together with the green onions and carrot. Combine the ingredients for the dressing and add to the vegetables. Toss well, then spoon into a serving dish. Sprinkle with toasted pine nuts or sesame seeds and serve.

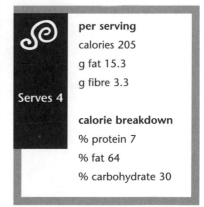

Serves 4

per serving
calories 205
g fat 15.3
g fibre 3.3

calorie breakdown
% protein 7
% fat 64
% carbohydrate 30

The University of Salerno in Italy, the pioneering medical school, taught this rule for a happy life in old age: eat ginger and you will love and be loved as in your youth!

Chicken, Scallops, and Asparagus Salad

Adapted from *Jane Brody's Good Food Gourmet*

When we made this dish one dark winter day, we were persuaded spring had just blossomed in the kitchen.

3/4 lb	asparagus, tough ends trimmed	375 g
3	cloves garlic, peeled and minced	3
2 tbsp	ginger, grated	30 mL
2 to 4	fresh jalapeños, seeded and minced	2 to 4
1 lb	boneless, skinless chicken breasts, sliced diagonally into 1/2-inch (1.5 cm) pieces	500 g
salt and pepper to taste		
1 tsp	butter	5 mL
1 tbsp	peanut oil	15 mL
1/2 lb	scallops (cut in half if large)	250 g
1/4 cup	dry white wine	50 mL
1/4 cup	chicken broth	50 mL
2 tbsp	minced fresh parsley	30 mL
greens for lining platter		

🌀 Steam asparagus for 1 1/2 minutes, and refresh under cold water. Cut diagonally into 1-inch (2.5 cm) pieces and set aside.

🌀 In a small bowl, combine the garlic, ginger, and jalapeños. Set the bowl aside.

🌀 Pat the chicken pieces dry with paper towels, and season the chicken with salt and pepper.

🌀 In a wok or large skillet, heat the butter and oil, add the chicken, and sauté for 2 minutes or until the chicken is no longer pink. Stir in the reserved garlic mixture, scallops, and reserved asparagus, and sauté the ingredients, stirring for 1 minute. Add the wine, broth, and parsley, and cook over high heat, stirring them, for one minute. Transfer the solids with a slotted spoon to a serving platter lined with greens.

🌀 Cook the liquid remaining in the pan 1 minute longer, and pour the liquid over the chicken mixture. Let salad cool to room temperature before serving it on a bed of greens. This dish may also be served hot with rice instead of salad greens.

per serving
calories 258
g fat 6.7
g fibre 1.7

Serves 4

calorie breakdown
% protein 65
% fat 24
% carbohydrate 11

Vegetables

Almost any cooked vegetable is enhanced by minced fresh ginger. If you're short on time, bottled minced or puréed ginger, found in most grocery stores, makes a palatable substitute. Preserved with vinegar, soy bean oil, and salt, these bottled products add even more zing to your favourite vegetables.

Microwave Buttercup Squash

1	medium-size	
	buttercup squash	1
1 tbsp	grated ginger	15 mL
1 tbsp	butter	15 mL
salt and pepper to taste		

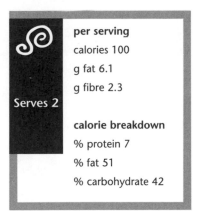

per serving
calories 100
g fat 6.1
g fibre 2.3

Serves 2

calorie breakdown
% protein 7
% fat 51
% carbohydrate 42

🌀 Cut unpeeled squash in half, horizontally. Scoop out seeds and strings with a spoon. Place one half of the squash on a small plate, cover with a paper towel, and microwave on high for 5 minutes, or until squash is well done. Repeat with the other squash half.

🌀 Scoop out the squash pulp into a large bowl and mash with a fork or masher. Add ginger, butter, salt, and pepper. Mix well.

🌀 If the squash has cooled, return it to the microwave for 1 or 2 minutes before serving.

Note: If you are in a hurry, leave the squash in the skins, mash it with a fork and add ginger, butter, salt, and pepper.

Spicy Green Beans and Carrots

Adapted from Jurgen Gothe's *Some Acquired Tastes: A Recipe Album*

As avid CBC listeners of DiscDrive, we are pleased to include this wonderful Ethiopian recipe from Jurgen Gothe's collection.

1 lb	fresh green beans, ends snipped and snapped into 2-inch (5 cm) pieces	500g
oil for sautéeing		
1	large onion, chopped	1
1	jalapeño pepper, seeded and chopped	1
3	medium garlic cloves, chopped	3
1 tbsp	ginger, chopped	15 mL
1 tsp	Hungarian paprika	5 mL
cayenne to taste		
1/2 tsp	cinnamon	2 mL
1/4 tsp	ground cloves	1 mL
1/2 tsp	turmeric	2 mL
pinch of freshly ground nutmeg		
1 lb	carrots cut into 2-inch (5 cm) lengths	500 g
salt to taste		
1 1/2 cups cold water		375 mL
2 tbsp	tomato paste	30 mL
green onions, chopped		
plain yogurt		

🌀 Blanch the beans by first filling a large pot with salted water and bring to a boil. Add beans and boil for 3 minutes. Drain and rinse with cold water.

🌀 In a large pan, heat oil and add onion. Cook over medium heat for 10 minutes, or until golden brown.

🌀 Add jalapeño pepper, garlic, ginger, and all the spices, then cook on low for 2 or 3 minutes.

🌀 Add the carrots, salt, and 1 cup (250 mL) of the water and simmer. Cover the pan and cook on low for 10 to 12 minutes.

🌀 Add tomato paste mixed with a little water. Heat through. Add more water if needed, though sauce should be quite thick. If too thin take lid off and simmer for a couple of minutes. Add the beans to the sauce and heat through.

🌀 Garnish with chopped green onions and a dollop of yogurt on each serving.

per serving
calories 163
g fat 4.6
g fibre 6.4

calorie breakdown
% protein 12
% fat 23
% carbohydrate 65

Serves 4

Fiddleheads with Ginger Coins

Fresh fiddleheads, the tips of the fern, are only available for a very short time each spring. Add ginger to these tasty morsels and you have a vegetable "to die for."

1 lb	fiddleheads	500 g
2 inches	ginger cut into thin coins	5 cm
lemon juice and zest from 1/2 a lemon		
2 tbsp	butter	30 mL

🌀 Wash fiddleheads and remove brown casings.

🌀 Steam fiddleheads until bright green and just tender.

🌀 Add coins of ginger, lemon juice and zest, and butter. Toss together and serve immediately.

per serving
calories 82.2
g fat 6.3
g fibre 0.8

calorie breakdown
% protein 14
% fat 60
% carbohydrate 26

Serves 4

Asparagus with Ginger and Lemon Butter Sauce

A winning starter when the asparagus is fresh, this dish never disappoints dinner guests. Have plenty of warm crusty bread available for sopping up the butter sauce.

1 lb	fresh asparagus	500g
3 tbsp	unsalted butter	45 mL
2 tsp	ginger juice*	10 mL
2 tbsp	lemon juice	30 mL
1 tsp	lemon zest	5 mL

salt, freshly grated pepper, and nutmeg to taste.

*See page viii

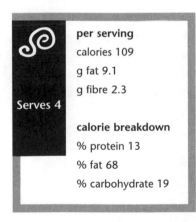

per serving
calories 109
g fat 9.1
g fibre 2.3

Serves 4

calorie breakdown
% protein 13
% fat 68
% carbohydrate 19

Wash and cut off tough ends of asparagus spears. Using a wide skillet to hold the asparagus flat, arrange asparagus with tops pointing in one direction. Pour in boiling water to barely cover the asparagus. Cover the pan and simmer until just tender.

While the asparagus is steaming, prepare the sauce by melting butter in a pan over medium heat. Add the ginger juice, lemon juice and zest, along with salt, pepper, and nutmeg to taste.

Drain asparagus and arrange on heated serving plates. Pour sauce over the asparagus and serve.

Vegetables such as peas, beans, broccoli, and carrots, take on new character when boiled in a weak ginger broth made from 3 tbsp (45 mL) coarsely chopped ginger and 4 cups (1 L) water, boiled for 15 minutes. If you are a vegetable fancier, it is a good idea to keep a supply of ginger broth in the refrigerator just for this purpose.

Spinach with Ginger and Cardamom

If you're not a fan of spinach, this recipe from Gillian Thomas just may sway you to enjoy it.

1 lb	spinach	500 g
2 tbsp	butter	30 mL
1/2 tsp	ground ginger	2 mL
2 tbsp	ginger, grated	30 mL
1 tsp	ground cardamom	5 mL

Wash and drain the spinach and remove tough stems. Set aside to dry.

Melt butter in a frying pan over medium heat. Add ground and grated ginger and cardamom, and sauté for 2 or 3 minutes. Add spinach and stir-fry for 3 or 4 minutes, or until limp but not overcooked. Serve as a bed for fish such as salmon or halibut, or as an accompaniment for the Chicken in Ginger Sauce (see page 65).

per serving
calories 81.9
g fat 6.3
g fibre 3.2

Serves 4

calorie breakdown
% protein 16
% fat 62
% carbohydrate 22

Eggplant with Tomatoes and Ginger

Eggplant, like tofu, absorbs and enhances the flavours of other ingredients. This traditional favourite is especially good if you can use Italian tomatoes, which are known by good chefs everywhere for their "character." With a glass of chilled white wine and crusty bread, this dish makes a memorable culinary event.

1/2 cup	chopped onion	125 mL
1 tbsp	olive oil	15 mL
1/4 cup	tomato paste	50 mL
4	Italian tomatoes, chopped	4
1 tbsp	minced ginger	15 mL
1	garlic clove, finely chopped	1
salt and freshly ground pepper to taste		
1	small eggplant (about 2 cups/500 mL)	1
olive oil for brushing eggplant (about 1 tbsp/15 mL)		
1 cup	yogurt	250 mL
cilantro for garnish		

In a saucepan, sauté the onion in 1 tbsp (15 mL) olive oil for about 5 minutes. Add the tomato paste, tomatoes, ginger, garlic, salt, and freshly ground black pepper. Cover and simmer for about 20 minutes.

While the sauce is simmering, slice the eggplant 1 inch (2.5 cm) thick, brush with olive oil, and place on a baking sheet. Cover with aluminum foil and bake in a preheated oven at 425°F (220°C) for 15 minutes. Turn each slice and cook for another 10 or 15 minutes, or until the eggplant is cooked through.

Place eggplant slices in a serving dish and spoon hot tomato sauce over them. Top with yogurt and garnish with cilantro.

per serving
calories 190
g fat 9.4
g fibre 5.7

Serves 4

calorie breakdown
% protein 13
% fat 42
% carbohydrate 46

Cabbage with Wakame Seaweed

Wakame seaweed is a common ingredient in Japanese cookery. Available in many specialty stores, it adds nutrients, texture, and a unique flavour to soups, salads, and stews. This combination of cabbage and Wakame seaweed makes a perfect companion to steamed fish, or try it on its own as a cold salad.

2 1/2 cups	cabbage	625 mL
1	6-inch (15 cm) length	
	Wakame seaweed	1
1 tbsp	soy sauce	15 mL
2 tsp	fish sauce	10 mL
2 tsp	grated ginger	10 mL
2 tsp	rice vinegar or sake	10 mL

Cut the cabbage into bite-size pieces and cook until tender. Drain and set aside.

Restore the seaweed by pouring boiling water over it. Drain immediately and immerse in cold water. Drain again and squeeze out excess water.

Spread out the restored seaweed and cut off the tough vein. Cut the softened sections into bite-size pieces. Add to the cabbage.

Mix together soy sauce, fish sauce, grated ginger, and rice vinegar or sake. Carefully toss with the cabbage and Wakame seaweed and serve immediately or, if using as a salad, chill for 1/2 hour in the refrigerator.

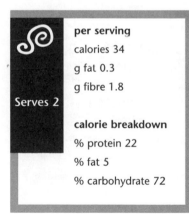

per serving
calories 34
g fat 0.3
g fibre 1.8

Serves 2

calorie breakdown
% protein 22
% fat 5
% carbohydrate 72

Note: When cooking with Wakame seaweed, a little goes a long way: it expands 7 to 8 times its dry volume when placed in boiling water.

In 1954, Sir Robert Perkins gave a speech in the British House of Commons complaining that its restaurant had not served the ginger-seasoned fowl dish "maupygernon" for the past 300 years.

Chickpea Vegetable Stir-Fry

Stir-fry vegetables are perfect dishes for today's busy lifestyles—fast, easy, and healthy. With chickpeas and cabbage, we feel doubly virtuous when we eat this spicy stir-fry.

1/2 cup	water	125 mL
2 tbsp	lime juice	30 mL
1 tbsp	lime zest	15 mL
1 tbsp	cornstarch	15 mL
1/2 tsp	ground ginger	2 mL
1/2 tsp	ground cumin	2 mL
1/2 tsp	cayenne	2 mL
1 tbsp	olive oil	15 mL
1 tsp	toasted sesame oil	5 mL
1	medium onion, sliced	1
2 inches	ginger, cut into thin coins	5 cm
2 cups	Savoy cabbage, shredded	500 mL
1/2	red pepper, chopped	1/2
4	green onions, sliced	4
2	cloves of garlic, minced	2
1 (19-oz)	can chickpeas, drained and rinsed	540 mL
fresh parsley or cilantro for garnish		

In a small bowl, combine water, lime juice and zest, cornstarch, and seasonings. Set aside.

In a skillet, heat olive and toasted sesame oils over medium high heat. Add onion, ginger coins, cabbage, red pepper, green onions, and garlic, and heat, stirring constantly, for about 3 minutes, or until just soft. Add chickpeas and heat, for 1 minute.

Add lime mixture to skillet and cook for about 2 minutes until thick, stirring constantly.

Serve over rice and sprinkle with parsley or cilantro.

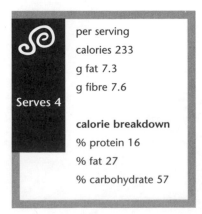

Serves 4

per serving
calories 233
g fat 7.3
g fibre 7.6

calorie breakdown
% protein 16
% fat 27
% carbohydrate 57

Baked Beans and Fruit

Adapted from Violet Curry and Kay Spicer's *Full of Beans*

Baked beans, traditionally served on Saturday night in Maritime homes, often contained a pinch of powdered ginger to aid digestion. Make this dish a day ahead to let the flavours mellow.

4 cups	cooked small red kidney beans, or Dutch brown beans	1 L
1	large onion, coarsely chopped	1
2	apples, peeled and chopped	2
2	navel oranges, peeled and sliced	2
1/3 cup	molasses or maple syrup	75 mL
1 tbsp	cider vinegar	15 mL
2 tbsp	ginger, minced	30 mL
2 tsp	Dijon mustard	10 mL
1/2 tsp	salt	2 mL
1/4 tsp	freshly ground black pepper	1 mL
1 tsp	hot pepper sauce	5 mL
hot water		

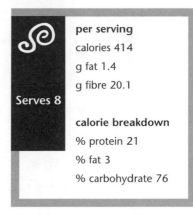

᷍ In an 8-cup (2 L) casserole, layer cooked beans, then onion, then apples; top with orange slices.

᷍ In a 2-cup (500 mL) measure, combine molasses, cider vinegar, ginger, mustard, salt, pepper, and hot pepper sauce. Add enough hot water to make 2 cups (500 mL) liquid. Mix well. Pour over bean mixture.

᷍ Cover and bake in preheated oven at 300°F (150°C) for about 1 hour, or until beans and fruit are tender. Uncover and stir. Bake, uncovered, for about 30 minutes longer, or until some of the liquid has evaporated.

per serving
calories 414
g fat 1.4
g fibre 20.1

Serves 8

calorie breakdown
% protein 21
% fat 3
% carbohydrate 76

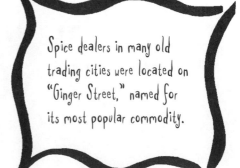

Spice dealers in many old trading cities were located on "Ginger Street," named for its most popular commodity.

Lemon and Ginger Spicy Beans

Adapted from *Ginger: A Book of Recipes*

*Canned beans transform this dish into a fast and easy
meal for the heartiest appetite.*

6 cups	cooked beans, preferably a mixture of black-eyed, adzuki, and northern beans	1.5 L
	or 3 (14-oz/400 g) cans of beans in three varieties	
2 tbsp	ginger, chopped	30 mL
3	garlic cloves, roughly chopped	3
1 cup	cold water	250 mL
1 tbsp	canola oil	15 mL
1	large onion, thinly sliced	1
1	fresh red chili, seeded and finely chopped	1
1/4 tsp	cayenne	1 mL
2 tsp	ground cumin	10 mL
1 tsp	ground coriander	5 mL
1/2 tsp	ground turmeric	2 mL
2 tbsp	lemon juice	30 mL
1/2 cup	chopped fresh coriander	125 mL

salt and freshly ground black
pepper to taste

🍥 Soak and cook the beans
separately, since they each take
slightly different cooking times or
use three varieties of canned
beans, drained and rinsed.

🍥 Place the ginger, garlic, and
4 tbsp (60 mL) of the cold water
in a blender or food processor
and blend until smooth. Set
aside.

🍥 Heat the oil in a pan. Add
the sliced onion and red chili and
cook gently for about 10 minutes
until softened and beginning to
caramelize. Add the cayenne,
cumin, coriander, and turmeric
and stir-fry for 1 minute.

🍥 Stir in the ginger and garlic
paste from the blender and cook
for another minute, stirring to
prevent sticking.

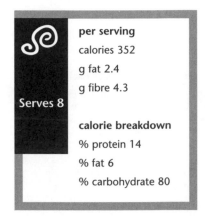

per serving	
calories 352	
g fat 2.4	
g fibre 4.3	
Serves 8	
calorie breakdown	
% protein 14	
% fat 6	
% carbohydrate 80	

🍥 Add the remaining water,
lemon juice, and fresh coriander,
stir well and bring to a boil.
Cover the pan tightly and cook
for 5 minutes. Add the beans and
cook for a further 5 to 10
minutes. Season with salt and
freshly ground black pepper to
taste.

Ginger is mentioned in Shakespeare's *Twelfth Night*:
Sir Toby: Dost thou think, because thou art virtuous, there shall be no
more cakes and ale?
Clown: Yes, by Saint Anne, and ginger shall be hot i', the mouth too.

Lentil Burgers

Adapted from Muriel Vibert's
Good Cooking with Natural Foods

*Vegetarian burgers take on new
character with ginger tossed in.*

Lentils

1 cup	lentils	250 mL
2 cups	water	500 mL
1	small onion,	
	finely chopped	1
1	medium carrot,	
	grated	1
2 tbsp	ginger, grated	30 mL
1 tbsp	oregano or thyme	15 mL
2 tsp	tamari	10 mL
3 tbsp	bulgur or quinoa	45 mL

Burger

2	green onions,	
	finely chopped	2
1	small carrot, grated	1
1 cup	large rolled oats	250 mL
1 tbsp	tamari	15 mL
3 tbsp	parsley, chopped	45 mL
3 tbsp	toasted sesame oil	45 mL

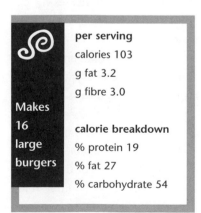

per serving
calories 103
g fat 3.2
g fibre 3.0

Makes 16 large burgers

calorie breakdown
% protein 19
% fat 27
% carbohydrate 54

🌀 Wash and drain lentils. In a pot, combine the water with the lentils, onion, carrot, ginger, and oregano or thyme. Cover and bring to a boil. Reduce heat and simmer for about 45 minutes, or until lentils are soft.

🌀 Add tamari and bulgur or quinoa. Cook for another 15 minutes. Leave cover off if the mixture seems too watery. Stir occasionally.

🌀 Remove from heat and cool. Mash, or use food processor, to purée half of the lentil mixture. Then add the purée to the other half of the lentil mixture along with green onions, carrot, rolled oats, tamari, and parsley. Mix well.

🌀 With wet hands, form the patties. They will hold together better if allowed to cool completely before frying. Fry the patties in toasted sesame oil. Turn only once.

Tofu Vegetable Stir-Fry

Tofu, healthy and an excellent source of protein, is perfect for capturing the flavours of stir-fry ingredients and marinades.

Marinade

2 tbsp	soy sauce	30 mL
2 tbsp	rice wine or	
	other white wine	30 mL
1	clove garlic, chopped	1
2 inches	ginger,	
	coarsely chopped	5 cm
12 oz	firm tofu, cut into 1-inch	
	(2.5 cm) cubes	375 mg

per serving
calories 339
g fat 19.7
f fibre 4.9
Serves 4
calorie breakdown
% protein 23
% fat 49
% carbohydrate 28

Stir-fry Ingredients

3 tbsp	toasted sesame oil	45 mL
2 inches	ginger, thinly sliced	5 cm
3	garlic cloves, chopped	3
2	leeks, thinly sliced	2
4	green onions,	
	finely chopped	4
1	red pepper,	
	cut into thin strips	1
1	yellow pepper	
	cut into thin strips	1
1 cup	cauliflower, broken	
	into small florets	250 mL
1 cup	broccoli, broken into	
	small florets	250 mL
1 cup	snow peas	250 mL
1 cup	white cabbage,	
	thinly sliced	250 mL
1/2 cup	purple cabbage,	
	thinly sliced	125 mL
1 tsp	Chinese five-spice	
	powder*	5 mL
1/2 tsp	salt	5 mL
zest of 1 lemon		

* Available in Asian food stores.

About 30 minutes before planning to eat, prepare marinade by mixing the soy sauce and wine; add garlic and ginger. Pour over tofu and stir carefully to coat it thoroughly. Set aside.

Wash and prepare stir-fry ingredients.

Heat 2 tbsp (30 mL) of sesame oil in a wok or large frying pan. Add ginger and garlic. When the oil begins to spit, add the vegetables, the five-star powder, and salt. Cook over high heat, stirring constantly, for about 3 minutes. Remove vegetables to a warmed dish.

Add 1 tbsp (15 mL) sesame oil to the pan. Drain the tofu and reserve the marinade. Fry the cubes of tofu over high heat, turning frequently (and carefully) until they are golden brown on all sides.

Remove tofu from the pan and return the vegetables to it for about 1 minute, or until the vegetables are steaming hot. Add the tofu, the reserved marinade, and the lemon zest. Stir and serve immediately.

Steamed Tofu Mould with Canadian Bacon

Adapted from Junko Lampert's *The Tofu Cookbook*

We like the Canadian bacon content of this highly original recipe.

Mould

12 oz	tofu	375 g
7 oz	Canadian bacon	175 g
6	large shiitake mushrooms	6
1	slice of carrot, cut from the base of a large carrot	1
1	scallion, chopped	1
2 tbsp	minced ginger	30 mL
2 tbsp	ginger, peeled and thinly sliced	30 mL
	vegetable oil	

Sauce

2 tbsp	broth from steaming the tofu	30 mL
1 tsp	cornstarch	5 mL
1 tsp	water	5 mL
1 tsp	soy sauce	5 mL
1 tsp	sake	5 mL
1 tsp	toasted sesame oil	5 mL

Cut tofu lengthwise into 1/4-inch (1 cm) thick rectangles. Separate pieces of Canadian bacon, which should be about 1 1/4 inches (3 cm) wide. Wash shiitake mushrooms, cut off stems, and cut into 1/2-inch (1 cm) strips. If using dried shiitake, soak in warm water for 15 minutes, or until soft. Cut the carrot slice in the shape of a flower, or use a decorative vegetable cutter to do the job.

For the mould, use a small Pyrex bowl with a diameter of about 8 inches (20 cm). Coat the inside of the bowl with vegetable oil. Place the carrot flower at the centre of the bottom of the bowl. Then line the bowl with strips of tofu, mushrooms, and bacon alternately. Fill the bowl with the remaining tofu, mushrooms, bacon, and add minced ginger. Sprinkle the top with chopped scallion and sliced ginger.

Place in a steamer, and steam over high heat for 20 minutes.

To make the sauce, gently pour 2 tbsp (30 mL) of the broth out of the bowl. In a separate bowl, dissolve cornstarch in the water. Combine broth in a small saucepan with all other sauce ingredients. Bring to a boil, stirring constantly.

Unmould the contents by inverting the bowl onto a serving dish. Pour the sauce over it and serve. This mixture does not melt together, but it does hold its shape after steaming.

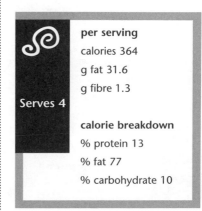

per serving
calories 364
g fat 31.6
g fibre 1.3

Serves 4

calorie breakdown
% protein 13
% fat 77
% carbohydrate 10

Tofu with Hoisin Sauce

Adapted from *Weight Watchers Healthy Life-Style Cookbook*

1/2 cup	sweet red pepper strips	125 mL
1/2 cup	chopped celery	125 mL
1 1/2 tsp	vegetable oil	7 mL
1 tbsp	ginger, minced	15 mL
1	clove garlic, minced	1
2 tbsp	dry sherry	30 mL
2 tsp	hoisin sauce	10 mL
1 tsp	soy sauce	5 mL
1 tsp	toasted sesame oil	5 mL
1/2 lb	tofu, cut into cubes	250 g
1/2 cup	sliced green onions	125 mL

In a microwave casserole, combine pepper, celery, oil, ginger, and garlic. Stir to coat. Microwave on high for 2 minutes.

Add sherry, hoisin sauce, soy sauce, and sesame oil. Stir and microwave on high for 1 minute. Add tofu, microwave for 1 minute; sprinkle with onions. Serve with whole wheat pita bread or on salad greens.

per serving
calories 152
g fat 8.8
g fibre 1.2

Serves 4

calorie breakdown
% protein 28
% fat 51
% carbohydrate 21

Tofu with Sweet Ginger Marinade

Adapted from Annie Somerville's *Fields of Greens: New Vegetarian Recipes from the Celebrated Greens Restaurant*

Delicious and versatile, this tangy dish elicits groans of appreciation every time. We are grateful to Heather Pierce for recommending it.

1 lb	firm tofu	500 g
1/2 cup	soy sauce or tamari	125 mL
3/4 cup	water	175 mL
1/2 cup	dry white wine or sweet cooking sake	125 mL
1/3 cup	sugar	75 mL
1/4 cup	dark sesame oil	50 mL
1/2 oz	dried shiitake mushrooms (optional)	12 g
1 1/2 tsp	dry mustard	7 mL
2 tbsp	ginger, grated	30 mL
4	cloves garlic, crushed with the side of a knife	4

Slice the tofu block in half horizontally or cut into slabs 1 inch thick. Place in a colander and drain for 10 to 15 minutes.

While the tofu is draining, prepare the marinade. Combine all other ingredients in a small saucepan. Bring to a boil, then reduce heat and simmer for 10 minutes.

per serving
calories 225
g fat 11.8
g fibre 0.3

Serves 6

calorie breakdown
% protein 18
% fat 50
% carbohydrate 33

Place the tofu in a square or rectangular saucepan. (A glass loaf pan is perfect for this recipe.) If the tofu is sliced, arrange the slices close together in the bottom of the pan or on top of one another in a double layer. Pour the hot marinade over the tofu to cover it completely. Cool, then cover with the lid or seal tightly with plastic wrap and refrigerate. For best results, marinate the tofu a full day before using.

The marinated tofu can be served fresh or grilled, accompanied by a dollop of Spicy Peanut Sauce (see page 9). It also makes a good filling for a sandwich.

Note: *The marinating tofu will last for a week or two in the refrigerator as long as it is well sealed. We also blended leftover tofu in a small amount of the marinade and used it as a dip for a tray of fresh vegetables.*

Ginger Cheese Soufflé with Herb Wine Sauce

Adapted from Anna Thomas' *The Vegetarian Epicure*

The sauce is the crowning glory to this heavenly dish. Have the eggs at room temperature when you begin to prepare the soufflé.

Soufflé

3 1/2 tbsp butter		50 mL
4 tbsp	flour	60 mL
1 1/2 cups milk		375 mL
2 tbsp	Dijon mustard	30 mL
2 tbsp	grated ginger	30 mL
1 tbsp	lemon zest	15 mL
pinch of cayenne		
salt and grated black pepper to taste		
2 tbsp	grated Parmesan	30 mL
3/4 cup	grated Swiss cheese	175 mL
6	egg yolks	6
8	egg whites	8
1/8 tsp	cream of tartar	0.5 mL

꩜ Prepare a soufflé dish by buttering it and making a "collar" of buttered greaseproof paper or tin foil that will extend 2 inches (5 cm) above the rim of the dish. Secure the collar by tying it with kitchen string just below the outside rim of the dish.

꩜ Melt butter in a saucepan and stir in the flour. Cook for a few minutes. Add milk, stirring with a whisk until you have a smooth, thick sauce.

꩜ Remove pan from heat and stir in mustard, ginger, lemon zest, cayenne, black pepper, salt, and cheeses.

꩜ When the sauce has cooled slightly, stir in the egg yolks with a whisk.

꩜ Add cream of tartar to the egg whites, and whip with an egg beater until stiff.

꩜ Stir a cup of the egg whites into the cheese mixture; this will lighten its texture. Fold in the remaining whites and pile the mixture carefully into the soufflé dish.

꩜ Place the dish in a preheated oven at 400°F (200°C) and turn the heat down to 375°F (190°C). Bake for 40 to 45 minutes.

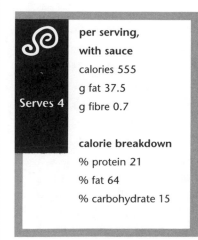

per serving, with sauce
calories 555
g fat 37.5
g fibre 0.7

Serves 4

calorie breakdown
% protein 21
% fat 64
% carbohydrate 15

Herb Wine Sauce

2 1/2 cups chicken or soy stock		625 mL
3/4 cup	white wine	175 mL
1/2 tsp	dried crumbled rosemary	2 mL
1 tsp	dried dill	5 mL
1/2 tsp	tarragon	2 mL
3 tbsp	butter	45 mL
3 tbsp	flour	45 mL
1/2 tsp	minced garlic	2 mL
1/2 tsp	lemon zest	2 mL
1/2 tsp	grated ginger	2 mL
salt and pepper to taste		

꩜ Cook the stock in a small saucepan until it is reduced by one half. (Cooks in a hurry can use a chicken or soy bouillon cube and less liquid to save cooking time here.) Add the wine and herbs. Simmer for 5 minutes.

꩜ Melt the butter in a heavy saucepan. Stir in the flour and simmer for 5 to 10 minutes, stirring constantly, until it begins to brown.

꩜ Gradually add the hot broth, stirring constantly. Season with garlic, lemon zest, ginger, salt, and pepper. Allow the sauce to simmer gently for another 10 to 15 minutes, stirring often.

꩜ Have ready to serve over the soufflé when it comes out of the oven.

Chinese Noodles with Green Curry

Adapted from Annie Somerville's *Fields of Greens: New Vegetarian Recipes from the Celebrated Greens Restaurant*

This is one of our favourite recipes, at its best when the greens are garden fresh. The curry and vegetables can be made before guests arrive, leaving only the noodles and assembly of this attractive dish to the last minute.

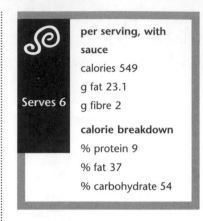

per serving, with sauce
calories 549
g fat 23.1
g fibre 2

Serves 6

calorie breakdown
% protein 9
% fat 37
% carbohydrate 54

Curry

6 oz	canned coconut milk	175 mL
3	green onions, white and green parts, cut into 1-inch (2.5 cm) lengths	3
2	jalapeño peppers, stems and seeds removed	2
2	garlic cloves, coarsely chopped	2
1/8 tsp	cayenne	0.5 mL
1 tsp	cumin seed, toasted and ground	5 mL
3 tbsp	fresh lemon juice (about 2 lemons)	45 mL
2 tbsp	peanut oil	30 mL
2 inches	ginger, julienned	5 cm
1 cup	firmly packed watercress sprigs, stems removed	250 mL
1 cup	firmly packed cilantro leaves, stems removed	250 mL
1/2 cup	firmly packed fresh mint leaves, stems removed	125 mL

Pour the coconut milk into a blender or food processor. Add the rest of the ingredients except the watercress, cilantro, and mint; purée until smooth.

Add all of the greens and purée, adding a little water if the curry is too thick. Do not over blend. Set aside.

Vegetables and Noodles

1 tsp	salt	5 mL
1/2 cup	snow peas, strings removed, thinly sliced	125 mL
2	green onions, both white and green parts, thinly sliced on a diagonal	2
1/2 cup	daikon radish cut into matchstick-size strips	125 mL
2	jalapeño peppers, seeded and thinly sliced	2
2 inches	fresh ginger	5 cm
1 16-oz	package fresh thin Chinese noodles (thin mein) or angel hair pasta	500 g
2 tbsp	peanut oil	30 mL
1/2 tsp	salt	2 mL
1 tbsp	chopped cilantro	15 mL
1/2 cup	toasted cashews	125 mL
watercress or cilantro sprigs for garnish		

Set a large pot of water on the stove to boil. When the water boils add 1 tsp (5 mL) salt. Add snow peas and cook for about 30 seconds, so that they are crisp and bright green. Scoop them from the water, rinse under cold water, and drain. Place them in a small bowl and toss with the green onions, daikon, and jalapeños. Set aside. Keep the water boiling.

Slice the ginger into thin coins, then into thin strips to make ginger threads.

Drop the noodles into the boiling water, giving them a quick stir and separating them so that they do not stick together. Cook for 3 or 4 minutes. Be sure they are just tender when they are pulled from the water. Drain noodles in a colander, rinse with cold water, and shake them to remove excess water. Toss with peanut oil, ginger threads, and 1/2 tsp (2 mL) salt.

Place the noodles on a platter or in a large salad bowl. Pour the curry over the noodles and arrange vegetables on top and greens around the edges. Sprinkle with chopped cilantro and cashews. Garnish with watercress or cilantro sprigs. Serve immediately.

Variation: *For a more hearty meal and added colour add 1/2 lb (250 g) of cold cooked shrimp along with the vegetables.*

Egg Noodles with Prosciutto, Melon, and Ginger

Originally created from leftovers in Margaret's refrigerator, the result was so good we keep our refrigerators stocked with these ingredients to satisfy urgent cravings.

16 oz	egg noodles	500 g
1/4 cup	ginger, minced	50 mL
1/2 cup	packed, chopped cilantro	125 mL
2	green onions, including tops, chopped	2
1/2 cup	cantaloupe, finely diced	125 mL
1/2 cup	thinly sliced prosciutto, chopped	125 mL
juice and zest of one lime		
2 tbsp	spicy ginger oil	30 mL
1/4 cup	grated Parmesan cheese or to taste	50 mL

Cook noodles in boiling water, according to package directions.

Meanwhile, chop ginger, cilantro, green onions, cantaloupe, and prosciutto. Prepare lime zest and juice.

Drain the noodles and place in a serving dish. Toss with spicy ginger oil, lime juice, and zest. Fold in remaining chopped ingredients and sprinkle with Parmesan cheese. Serve on heated plates.

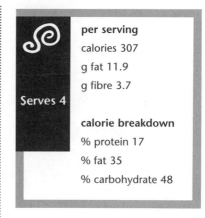

Serves 4

per serving
calories 307
g fat 11.9
g fibre 3.7

calorie breakdown
% protein 17
% fat 35
% carbohydrate 48

This dish makes a great cold salad.

Soba Noodles with Ginger Sesame Dressing

The Japanese are fond of a hearty buckwheat noodle called soba that can now be found in many specialty stores in North America. Although this recipe traditionally calls for dashi, a stock made of fish and kelp, chicken or soy stock can be used instead to make the dipping sauce.

1/2 cup	soy sauce	125 mL
2 tbsp	dashi, chicken,	
	or soy stock	30 mL
1 tsp	sugar	5 mL
1 tsp	finely grated ginger	5 mL
2 tbsp	toasted sesame seeds	30 mL
1/2 lb	soba	250 g
3	green onions, cut	
	diagonally into 1-inch	
	(2.5 cm) pieces	3

In a food processor, combine soy sauce, stock, sugar, ginger, and 1 tbsp (15 mL) toasted sesame seeds, and blend until smooth. Set aside.

Cook noodles according to package directions until they are done but still firm. Drain and toss in a bowl with the dressing. Allow to cool to room temperature. Add green onions, garnish with remaining 1 tbsp (15 mL) toasted sesame seeds.

per serving
calories 137
g fat 3.7
g fibre 0.3

Serves 4

calorie breakdown
% protein 22
% fat 23
% carbohydrate 55

Variation: To make a more substantial cold salad, toss in 1/2 lb (250 g) of fresh asparagus or green beans, cooked until just al dente and chopped in 1-inch (2.5 cm) pieces.

Steamed White Fish

A classic Chinese recipe, steamed fish is delicious and easy to prepare. It is useful to have a large Chinese basket steamer at least 12 inches (30 cm) in diameter or a metal steamer. Some recipes suggest marinating the fish in a mixture of wine, vinegar, and soy sauce, then decorating it with strips of shredded ham, bacon, dried mushrooms, spring onions, and ginger before steaming. This is a simpler version, but it is still essential to use fresh fish. We prefer white fish such as red snapper or sea bass, but have successfully steamed small trout and salmon this way. Although whole fish is most commonly used, fish fillets can be used with good results.

1	whole white fish,	
	1 1/2 lbs (750 g)	1
1 tsp	salt	5 mL
2 tsp	soy sauce	10 mL
1 tbsp	Shao hsing or	
	dry sherry	15 mL
1 1/2 tbsp	peanut or	
	vegetable oil	22 mL
pinch of sugar		
2 tbsp	ginger, grated	30 mL
8	coins of ginger, about 1 inch	
	(2.5 cm), thinly sliced	8
3	green onions, slivered	3
sprigs of fresh coriander for garnish		

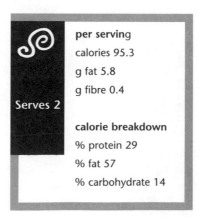

per serving
calories 95.3
g fat 5.8
g fibre 0.4

Serves 2

calorie breakdown
% protein 29
% fat 57
% carbohydrate 14

🌀 Rinse the fish and dry thoroughly. Rub salt over the entire fish inside and out.

🌀 Combine the soy sauce, wine or sherry, peanut or vegetable oil, sugar, and grated ginger. Set aside.

🌀 Pour enough water into the steamer or wok to come within an inch of the cooking rack. Cover and bring to a boil.

🌀 Put fish on a heat-proof platter, pour sauce over it, and decorate with coins of ginger and slivers of green onion. Place lengths of green onion on top.

🌀 Steam for 15 minutes or until the fish is just firm to the touch.

🌀 Garnish with coriander and serve with rice to soak up the sauce.

Gingered Codfish Cakes

Fish cakes are becoming fashionable in gourmet restaurants these days but you don't need to pay gourmet prices to enjoy them.

1 lb	dried salt cod	500 g
3 1/2 cups	mashed potatoes	875 mL
2 tbsp	butter	30 mL
1 tbsp	ginger, grated	15 mL
1/2 cup	onion, chopped	125 mL
1/2 cup	green onions, finely chopped	125 mL
1	egg	1
1 tbsp	cream or more to obtain desired consistency	15 mL

𝕊 Soak dried cod overnight in cold water. Change water, remove any bones and simmer for 15 minutes, or until soft. Drain fish and reserve.

𝕊 In a skillet melt butter and sauté ginger and onions until soft and beginning to brown.

𝕊 Combine all ingredients in a large bowl, blending thoroughly.

𝕊 Shape mixture into individual patties and pan-fry in a buttered skillet until heated through. Serve with rhubarb or ginger relish (see page 13).

Mussels with Ginger–Soy Dressing

Adapted from Shinko Shimizu's *New Salads: Quick Healthy Recipes from Japan*

The secret to this scrumptious dish is fresh mussels … and a hint of sake.

1 lb	mussels in their shells	500 g
1/2 tsp	salt	2 mL
1 tbsp	sake	15 mL
1 tsp	ginger juice*	5 mL
1 tsp	soy sauce	5 mL
1	lemon, sliced in thin quarter rounds	1
1/4 cup	chopped cilantro	50 mL
*See page viii		

𝕊 Wash the mussel shells thoroughly and transfer to a saucepan. Sprinkle with salt and sake. Cover and place over medium heat. Steam until the shells open, about 5 minutes. Discard any mussels that do not open.

𝕊 While mussels are steaming combine ginger juice and soy sauce. About 30 seconds after the shells open in the saucepan, add the sauce and stir well. Remove from heat.

𝕊 Transfer the mussels to a serving dish, pour sauce from pan over the mussels and garnish with lemon and chopped cilantro.

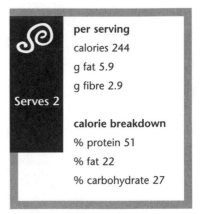

per serving
calories 244
g fat 5.9
g fibre 2.9

Serves 2

calorie breakdown
% protein 51
% fat 22
% carbohydrate 27

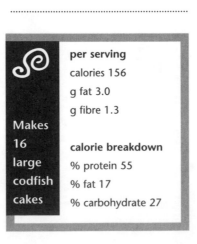

per serving
calories 156
g fat 3.0
g fibre 1.3

Makes 16 large codfish cakes

calorie breakdown
% protein 55
% fat 17
% carbohydrate 27

Goan Style Mussels

This sauce for mussels is thick and flavourful enough to make an appetizing main course served over rice. In smaller amounts, and with lots of crusty bread to soak up the sauce, it also makes a tantalizing starter for any meal. We are indebted to Joyce Balfour for this amazing recipe.

2 lbs	mussels	1 kg
2 inches	ginger, chopped	5 cm
8	cloves of garlic, chopped	8
1/2 cup	water	125 mL
4 tbsp	vegetable oil	60 mL
2	large onions, peeled and chopped	2
2	jalapeño peppers, thinly sliced	2
1/2 tsp	ground turmeric	2 mL
2 tsp	ground cumin seeds	10 mL
1 cup	grated fresh coconut	250 mL
1/2 tsp	salt	2 mL
1 cup	water	250 mL

෨ Clean mussels by washing them under cold water.

෨ Purée ginger and garlic with 1/2 cup (125 mL) of water until smooth.

෨ Heat oil in a large pot over medium heat. Sauté onions until translucent. Add the ginger and garlic purée, jalapeño peppers, turmeric, and cumin seeds. Stir-fry for 1 minute.

෨ Add coconut, salt, and 1 cup (250 mL) of water. This mixture may be prepared in advance up to this point.

෨ Bring mixture to a boil. Add mussels and mix well. Cover tightly, lower heat slightly and let mussels steam for 6 to 10 minutes, or until open. Serve immediately.

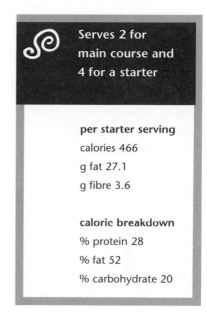

Serves 2 for main course and 4 for a starter

per starter serving
calories 466
g fat 27.1
g fibre 3.6

caloric breakdown
% protein 28
% fat 52
% carbohydrate 20

Pan-Fried Scallops with Ginger Dipping Sauce

In the Maritimes, scallops are traditionally fried to perfection, served with or without a dash of lemon. The dipping sauce with this recipe brings out even more of the flavour of this versatile seafood.

Dipping Sauce

5 tbsp	dry sherry	75 mL
2 tbsp	soy sauce	30 mL
1 tbsp	minced ginger	15 mL
1	garlic clove, finely chopped	1
1 tsp	sesame oil	5 mL
1 tbsp	green onion, finely chopped	15 mL
dash chili sauce		

Scallops

1 lb	Digby scallops, sliced in 1/2-inch (2 cm) coins	500 g
2 tbsp	unsalted butter	30 mL

In a small bowl, combine the dipping sauce ingredients and set aside.

Melt 1 tbsp (15 mL) butter over high heat. When butter is hot, add half the scallops and cook until they are opaque and lightly golden on both sides. Be careful not to overcook—the key to the flavour is the browning. Place cooked scallops on a warm platter and repeat the process with the remaining butter and scallops.

Transfer scallops to warm plates or scallop shells. Serve dipping sauce in individual small bowls to accompany the scallops.

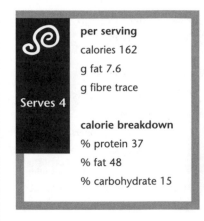

Serves 4

per serving
calories 162
g fat 7.6
g fibre trace

calorie breakdown
% protein 37
% fat 48
% carbohydrate 15

Foil-Baked Scallops with Ginger, Mushrooms, and Water Chestnuts

Baking in foil packets allows the scallops to absorb the succulent flavours of their companions. For a more elegant dinner party, use parchment paper instead of foil.

1 tsp	garlic, minced	5 mL
2 tbsp	butter, melted	30 mL
1/4 cup	green onion, thinly sliced	50 mL
1 tsp	ginger, grated	5 mL
1 tsp	lemon zest	5 mL
1 cup	mushrooms, sliced	250 mL
1/3 cup	thinly sliced water chestnuts	75 mL
1 tbsp	lemon juice	15 mL
salt and pepper to taste		
1 tsp	toasted sesame oil, plus additional oil for brushing foil	5 mL
3/4 lb	large Digby scallops, halved horizontally	375 g
1 tbsp	fresh coriander, minced	15 mL

per serving
calories 158
g fat 7.8
g fibre 0.7

Serves 4

calorie breakdown
% protein 41
% fat 44
% carbohydrate 14

In a heavy skillet cook the garlic in the butter over moderately low heat, stirring for 1 minute. Add the green onion, ginger, and zest and cook the mixture, stirring, for 1 minute. Add the mushrooms and water chestnuts, and cook, stirring, for 2 or 3 minutes, or until all the liquid the mushrooms give off is evaporated. Stir in the lemon juice and salt and pepper to taste.

Cut 2 pieces of 12 x 20 inch (30 x 50 cm) foil, and fold each in half—with the shiny side in—by bringing the short ends together. Unfold each piece, brush the centre with the additional sesame oil. Arrange half the scallops, seasoned with salt and pepper, just to one side of the fold line, and top the scallops with the vegetable mixture. Sprinkle each serving with 1/2 tsp (2 mL) of the remaining oil and 1 1/2 tsp (7 mL) of the coriander. Fold the edges together to form tightly sealed packets.

Bake the packets on a baking sheet in the middle of a preheated oven at 450°F (220°C) for 10 minutes.

Transfer the packets to plates and slit them open at the table or alternatively open them carefully, transfer the scallops to plates and pour the juices over them, discarding the foil. Serve with bread or rice.

Scallops with Black Beans and Ginger—Chili Oil

Adapted from Janet Hazen's *Hot, Hotter, Hottest: 50 Fiery Recipes From Around the World*

This mouth-watering recipe is not for the faint-hearted—watch out for those chilies!

Ginger—Chili Oil

1/2 cup	peanut oil	125 mL
4	dried chilies, crushed	4
1/2 cup	ginger, minced	125 mL
2	cloves garlic, thinly sliced	2
2 tbsp	toasted sesame oil	30 mL
2 tbsp	soy sauce	30 mL

In a heavy-bottom skillet, heat peanut oil, chilies, ginger, and garlic over moderate heat, stirring constantly for 2 minutes, or until it begins to sizzle. Add the sesame oil and soy sauce and cook for 2 minutes.

Remove from the heat and cool slightly. Strain through a fine wire mesh and set aside.

Scallops

2 tbsp	peanut oil	30 mL
1/2 cup	ginger, slivered	125 mL
1 lb	large Digby scallops	500 g
3 tbsp	preserved black beans	45 mL
3 tbsp	dry sherry	45 mL
1	large red pepper, julienned	1
2 cups	fresh spinach leaves or other greens	500 mL

About 5 minutes before serving time, heat the peanut oil in a wok or large nonstick pan.

When the oil is very hot, add ginger and scallops and cook for 2 minutes, stirring constantly. Add the black beans, sherry, and red pepper and cook for 1 minute, stirring constantly.

Remove from heat and arrange on top of spinach leaves (shredded green cabbage may be substituted), or serve with steamed rice. Drizzle with Ginger-Chili Oil and serve immediately.

per serving
calories 286
g fat 15.0
g fibre 1.6

Serves 4

calorie breakdown
% protein 34
% fat 49
% carbohydrate 16

Dioscorides, surgeon to emperors Claudius and Nero, wrote in 77 AD that ginger "warms and softens the stomach."

Ginger and Bourbon Shrimp on Snow Peas

Easy to make, this five-star recipe yields one of the most memorable meals in our ginger repertoire. The combination of bourbon and Grand Marnier transforms snow peas and shrimp into an out-of-body experience.

1/2 cup	ginger, slivered	125 mL
3/4 cup	water	175 mL
2 tbsp	shallots, minced	30 mL
3 tbsp	unsalted butter	45 mL
1 1/2 lbs	jumbo shrimp, shelled and deveined	750 g
1/2 tsp	rosemary, crumbled	2 mL
1/2 tsp	dried thyme, crumbled	2 mL
2 tbsp	bourbon	30 mL
1 tbsp	Grand Marnier	15 mL
1/2 cup	fish or chicken stock	125 mL
2/3 cup	heavy cream	150 mL
3/4 lb	snow peas, trimmed, blanched in boiling salt water for 30 seconds and drained	375 g
salt and pepper to taste		

per serving
calories 357
g fat 17.3
g fibre 2.29

Serves 4

calorie breakdown
% protein 39
% fat 47
% carbohydrate 14

In a small saucepan combine the ginger and water, bring to a boil, and simmer the mixture for 10 minutes. Drain the ginger, reserving it and 3 tbsp (45 mL) of the cooking liquid separately. Set aside.

In a large heavy skillet, cook the shallots in 2 tbsp (30 mL) of the butter over moderately low heat, stirring occasionally, until they are golden. Increase the heat to moderately high, and add the shrimp, the rosemary, and thyme. Sauté the mixture, stirring, for 3 minutes, or until the shrimp are just firm to the touch, and transfer the shrimp with a slotted spoon to a bowl.

Add the bourbon and the Grand Marnier to the skillet carefully and deglaze the skillet over moderately high heat, scraping up the brown bits. Add the reserved ginger cooking liquid and the stock and boil the liquid until there is only enough left to coat the bottom of the skillet. Add the cream and simmer the mixture until it is reduced by half.

While the cream mixture is being reduced, in another large skillet cook the blanched snow peas in the remaining 1 tbsp (15 mL) of butter over moderately low heat, stirring occasionally, until they are heated through. Add salt and pepper to taste.

Add to the reduced cream mixture the shrimp, any juices that have accumulated in the bowl, and the reserved ginger. Cook the mixture over moderately low heat, stirring occasionally, until it is heated through. Arrange the snow peas decoratively on four heated plates and mound the shrimp mixture on them. Serve immediately.

Sautéed Salmon Fillets with Bok Choy

After a hard day at work, this dish is a godsend. It is easy to make and pleasing to both the eye and the palate. We prefer the nutty flavour of bok choy, but any green can be used to show off the salmon.

2 lbs	bok choy or	
	other greens	1 kg
8	salmon fillets	8
1/2 cup	unsalted butter	25 mL
1	large onion, chopped	1
2	cloves garlic, minced	2
1 tbsp	ginger, minced	15 mL
1 tbsp	olive oil	15 mL
3 tbsp	lemon juice	45 mL
3 tbsp	parsley	45 mL

salt and freshly ground black pepper to taste

per serving, for 8
calories 429
g fat 26.3
g fibre 2.3

Serves 4 or 8

calorie breakdown
% protein 38
% fat 55
% carbohydrate 7

Wash the bok choy or other greens thoroughly, remove tough stems, and chop leaves with a large knife.

Rinse salmon under cold water and pat dry with a paper towel. Place each fillet between 2 pieces of waxed paper or foil and pound very lightly to obtain an even thickness. Season to taste with salt and pepper.

Heat 3 tbsp (45 mL) of the butter in a skillet over medium-high heat. Add the onion, garlic, and ginger, and sauté until onions are soft but not brown, about 4 minutes. Stir in the greens and sauté for about 3 minutes, or until the greens are just tender. Remove from heat and keep warm.

Heat 2 tbsp (30 mL) of the butter and olive oil in the pan over medium-high heat. Sauté 3 or 4 salmon fillets at a time, cooking about 1 minute on each side. Do not overcook. Remove fillets and drain briefly on paper towels. Cook the remaining fillets, adding more oil and butter if necessary. When all the fillets are cooked, add the lemon juice to the pan, and scrape the bottom of the pan with a wooden spoon. Add the remaining butter and stir until melted. Stir in the parsley.

To serve, spread the greens equally on four warmed plates, covering the surfaces entirely. Top with 1 or 2 of the salmon fillets, pour the pan sauce over the fillets, and serve immediately.

Smoked Salmon Pasta with Gin, Ginger, and Green Onions

Our twist on a classic pasta tastes divine. Make it when you want to pamper yourself but are too busy to spend much time in the kitchen.

3 tbsp	butter	45 mL
1 tbsp	onion, finely chopped	15 mL
1	clove garlic, finely chopped	1
3 tbsp	ginger, finely chopped	45 mL
1/4 lb	smoked salmon, cut in strips	125 g
salt and freshly ground black pepper to taste		
1/4 cup	gin	50 mL
3	green onions, including green tops, finely chopped	3
1/2 cup	cream	125 mL
1 tsp	lemon zest	5 mL
1 lb	fettuccini or other plain pasta	500 g
1/2 cup	Parmesan cheese	125 mL

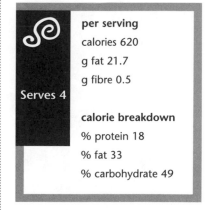

Melt butter in a saucepan over medium heat. Add onions, garlic, and ginger. Cook about 5 minutes.

Add salmon and salt and pepper to taste. Increase the heat to high and cook for 2 to 3 minutes, stirring constantly.

Pour in gin and reduce heat. Simmer until the liquid is reduced by half.

Add chopped green onions (reserving 1 tbsp/15 mL for garnish) and cream, and simmer until the cream is reduced and thickened slightly, about 5 minutes. Add lemon zest, mix thoroughly and remove from heat.

Meanwhile, cook fettuccini in a large pot of boiling water until tender but firm. Drain and place in a warmed serving bowl or on warmed individual plates.

Pour sauce on top of fettuccini, sprinkle with Parmesan cheese and reserved green onions, and serve.

per serving
calories 620
g fat 21.7
g fibre 0.5

Serves 4

calorie breakdown
% protein 18
% fat 33
% carbohydrate 49

Poached Ginger Salmon Steaks

Salmon and ginger seem to be meant for each other. This recipe is fit for a queen should you ever entertain royalty.

2 inches	ginger, thinly sliced	5 cm
1	large garlic clove, minced	1
1 tbsp	cracked black peppercorns	15 mL
2	lemon slices	2
2 tbsp	soy sauce	30 mL
1 cup	water	250 mL
2	salmon steaks, about 1/2 inch (1.5 cm) thick	2
1 tbsp	unsalted butter, cut into bits	15 mL
1 tbsp	fresh parsley leaves, minced	15 mL
salt to taste		

In a 2-qt (2 L) microwave-safe casserole with a lid combine the sliced ginger, garlic, peppercorns, lemon, soy sauce, and water. Microwave the mixture, uncovered, on high for 5 minutes.

Add the salmon in one layer to the cooking liquid. Microwave the mixture, covered, on medium for 5 to 7 minutes, or until the salmon just flakes. Transfer the salmon with a slotted spatula to 2 plates.

In a bowl whisk together 2 tbsp (30 mL) of the cooking liquid, butter, parsley, and salt to taste, and serve the sauce over the salmon.

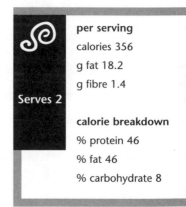

per serving
calories 356
g fat 18.2
g fibre 1.4

Serves 2

calorie breakdown
% protein 46
% fat 46
% carbohydrate 8

The following seventeenth-century ditty is found in *The Knight of the Burning Pestle:*

Nose, nose, jolly red nose,
And who gave thee this jolly red nose?
Nutmeg and ginger, cinnamon and cloves,
And they gave me this jolly red nose.

Lobster "Chinois" and Pan-Fried Noodle Cakes

Adapted from *Cooper's Inn Cookbook*

When Gary Hynes ran the kitchen at Cooper's Inn in Shelburne, Nova Scotia, he prepared some of the most imaginative food we have ever eaten. This recipe captures his flare for giving local ingredients an exotic twist. Lobster was never served like this when we were growing up.

Pan-Fried Noodle Cakes

8 oz	vermicelli or rice noodles	250 g
1 tbsp	unsalted butter	15 mL
1 tbsp	sesame oil	15 mL
1 tbsp	peanut or corn oil	15 mL

🌀 Bring to a boil a large pot of salted water. Cook the noodles according to directions on the package and drain but do not rinse. Immediately divide and form the noodles into 4 pancakes on a cookie sheet and let them cool.

🌀 In a large frying pan heat the butter and oils over medium-high heat. Sauté the noodle cakes, flipping with a spatula, until crispy brown. Keep warm in the oven until needed.

Lobster

1 lb	fresh, canned or frozen cooked lobster meat	500 g
4 tbsp	unsalted butter	60 mL
1/2 cup	sweet wine, port, or sweet sherry	125 mL
1/2 cup	fish or soy stock	125 mL
1/2 cup	heavy cream	125 mL
1 tsp	ground fenugreek	5 mL
2 tbsp	green onions, chopped	30 mL
2 tbsp	fresh cilantro, chopped	30 mL
1/4 tsp	cayenne	1 mL
1 tbsp	garlic, finely chopped	15 mL
1 tbsp	ginger, finely chopped	15 mL
1/2 cup	fresh cilantro, chopped	125 mL
chili oil		

🌀 Heat 2 tbsp (30 mL) of butter in a large saucepan until hot and quickly sauté the lobster to reheat it—1 or 2 minutes. Place a noodle cake on each plate and top with some of the lobster.

🌀 Deglaze the pan with the wine, and then add stock, cream, fenugreek, green onions, cilantro, cayenne, garlic, and ginger. Cook over high heat until the mixture is reduced by half. Remove from heat and whisk in 2 tbsp (30 mL) of butter. Spoon over the lobster. Sprinkle with the chopped cilantro and a little chili oil on top.

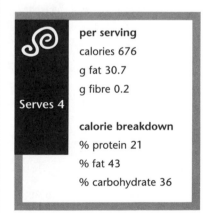

🌀 **Serves 4**

per serving
calories 676
g fat 30.7
g fibre 0.2

calorie breakdown
% protein 21
% fat 43
% carbohydrate 36

Wild Rice with Shrimp and Lobster

Adapted from Hugh Carpenter and Teri Sandison's *Hot Wok*

This is the perfect dish to serve on Canada Day, July 1, when lobster are plentiful and snow peas are available locally. Hot wok cooking requires good organization and timing, so line up your ingredients before heating the wok.

Hot Wok Ingredients

1/3 cup	pine nuts, toasted	175 mL
1 lb	cooked lobster meat, about 4 (1-lb/500 g) lobster or 1 lb (500 g) canned or frozen lobster meat	500 g
1/2 lb	medium-size shrimp, cooked	250 g
3	green onions	3
1 cup	snow peas	250 mL
3 oz	enoki mushrooms, if available, or button mushrooms	75 g
1/2 cup	fresh cilantro sprigs	125 mL
3 cups	cold cooked wild rice or a mixture of wild and white rice (cooked according to recipe)	750 mL
2 tbsp	cooking oil	30 mL
2 tbsp	butter	30 mL
3 tbsp	ginger, minced	45 mL
1/4 cup	water	50 mL

Hot Wok Sauce

1/4 cup	port	50 mL
1 tbsp	light soy sauce	15 mL
2 tbsp	oyster sauce	30 mL
2 tbsp	roasted sesame oil	30 mL
1 tbsp	red wine vinegar	15 mL
1 tsp	cornstarch	5 mL
1/2 tsp	Asian chili sauce	2 mL

Toast pine nuts in preheated oven at 325°F (170°C) until they become golden.

Meanwhile, place live lobster in boiling, slightly salted water and cook for 20 minutes. Run cold water over boiled lobster and when cool, remove meat from claws and tail. Set lobster meat aside in refrigerator, covered.

Shell and devein shrimp, then cut them deeply lengthwise and refrigerate.

Cut the green onions on a sharp diagonal into 1/4-inch (1 cm) slivers. Wash and pull the strings off snow peas. Combine the peas and onions in a small bowl. Discard the root ends from enoki mushrooms and pull apart. Chop the cilantro.

In separate containers, set aside mushrooms, chopped cilantro, cooked wild rice, cooking oil, butter, and water.

Combine Hot Wok Sauce ingredients and set aside.

Hot Wok Action

Place wok over the highest heat. When the wok becomes very hot, add the cooking oil to the centre. Roll the oil around the wok and when the oil gives off just a wisp of smoke add the shrimp. Stir and toss until it loses its raw outside colour, about 2 minutes, and then set the shrimp aside on a plate.

Immediately return the wok to the highest heat. Add the butter and the ginger. As soon as the butter melts, add the peas and green onions to the wok. Stir and toss, adding water so that the peas cook evenly, and turn bright green, about two minutes. Add the wild rice, mushrooms, pine nuts, lobster meat, and shrimp to the wok. Stir and toss to combine evenly, then add the Hot Wok Sauce. Stir and toss until the rice is thoroughly reheated, about 3 minutes. Stir in the cilantro. Taste and adjust the seasonings. Serve immediately.

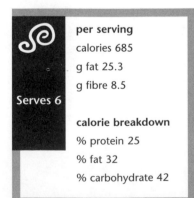

Serves 6

per serving
calories 685
g fat 25.3
g fibre 8.5

calorie breakdown
% protein 25
% fat 32
% carbohydrate 42

Meat
Meat
Meat
Meat
Meat
Meat
Meat
Meat

Chicken in Ginger Sauce

From his home in Lunenburg, Nova Scotia, Gerry Hallowell, an editor who works for the University of Toronto Press, serves up this fine nosh, which has become one of our favourite dishes.

4	chicken breasts, skinned & deboned	4
2 tbsp	vegetable oil	30 mL
6	green onions, finely chopped	6
3	cloves garlic	3
3 tbsp	ginger, grated	45 mL
1 tsp	ground cumin	5 mL
2 tsp	Garam Masala*	10 mL
salt and freshly ground black pepper to taste		
1 tbsp	lemon juice	15 mL
6 tbsp	hot water	90 mL
parsley sprigs and lemon slices for garnish		

	per serving
	calories 209
	g fat 8.6
	g fibre 0.9
Serves 4	
	calorie breakdown
	% protein 55
	% fat 38
	% carbohydrate 8

🌀 Pat the chicken dry and slice thinly.

🌀 Heat oil in a large skillet; add green onions and cook, stirring often, 2 or 3 minutes to soften. Remove green onions from pan with a slotted spoon and set aside.

🌀 Add chicken to skillet and cook over high heat, stirring frequently, for about 5 minutes, or until brown.

🌀 Stir in garlic, ginger, cumin, Garam Masala, salt, and pepper. Cook 1 minute, then stir in cooked green onions, lemon juice, and water. Cover and cook over low heat for about 10 minutes or until chicken is tender. Serve with rice or couscous, garnished with parsley and lemon slices.

*Garam Masala is a blend of dried spices combined and ground together for use as a seasoning in Indian cooking. Available in specialty stores, it includes a combination of cinnamon, cardamom, whole cloves, cumin seeds, coriander seeds, and black peppercorns.

Chicken Stuffed with Fruited Rice

This is Heather's idea of a hearty winter meal. Make enough stuffing for the chicken cavity and for a small casserole so there's plenty to go around.

1 cup	whole almonds, lightly roasted	250 mL
2 cups	rice (Manomin Mix* is especially good for this recipe)	500 mL
1 cup	bread, cut into 1-inch (2.5 cm) chunks	250 mL
2 tbsp	butter	30 mL
1	medium yellow onion, chopped	1
1	small apple, finely chopped	1
1	celery stalk, finely chopped	1
3 tbsp	ginger, grated	45 mL
2 cups	dried fruit mixture (apricots, raisins, prunes, cherries)	500 mL
1/4 tsp	ground cinnamon	1 mL
	freshly grated black pepper to taste	
1	large roasting chicken, 6 lbs (3 kg)	1

For basting:

1 tbsp	melted butter	15 mL
	zest and juice of 1 lemon	
1 tbsp	ginger, grated	15 mL

Roast almonds in preheated oven at 350°F (180°C) until lightly browned, about 7 minutes.

Cook the rice according to package instructions and cut up the bread.

To prepare the stuffing, heat the butter in a large frying pan. Sauté the onion, apple, celery, and ginger. Carefully stir in the dried fruit, almonds, cinnamon, and black pepper.

Remove from the heat and mix in the bread and rice.

Melt the basting butter and stir in the lemon juice.

Loosely stuff the chicken and close the ends with skewers or by trussing. Place the remaining dressing in a covered casserole. Tie the legs and wings close to the body of the chicken and place the chicken in a roasting pan. Rub the skin with the lemon zest and ginger. Spoon the lemon juice and butter mixture over the chicken.

Roast, covered, in preheated oven at 350°F (180°C) for 30 minutes per pound. Baste frequently. Remove cover for the last 30 minutes of cooking.

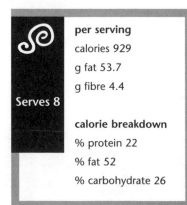

per serving
calories 929
g fat 53.7
g fibre 4.4

Serves 8

calorie breakdown
% protein 22
% fat 52
% carbohydrate 26

*Manomin Mix is a three-rice blend of Manomin wild, long grain white, and white basmati rice produced by Kagiwiosa Manamin, an Ojibway owned and operated cooperative located in Ontario.

Ginger Glazed Chicken

Bored with chicken? Dress it up with this easy recipe. Isabel Palmeter, a former Home Economics teacher, adapted this recipe to suit the constraints of time in her classroom.

4	chicken breasts or pieces	4
2 tbsp	canola oil	30 mL
3/4 cup	orange juice	175 mL
2 tbsp	soy sauce	30 mL
1 tbsp	ginger, grated	15 mL
1	clove garlic, chopped	1
zest of 1 orange		
2 tbsp	preserved ginger	30 mL

꩜ Fry the chicken pieces in oil or bake in preheated oven at 375°F (190°C).

꩜ While the chicken is cooking, mix the other ingredients to make a sauce. When the chicken is nearly cooked, pour the sauce over the chicken. Simmer for a few minutes, basting occasionally. Serve with rice and a green salad.

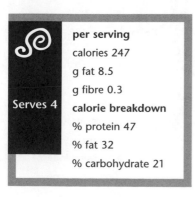

per serving
calories 247
g fat 8.5
g fibre 0.3
calorie breakdown
% protein 47
% fat 32
% carbohydrate 21

Serves 4

Buttermilk Marinated Chicken with Bacon, Blueberries, Ginger, and Sage

Adapted from *Cooper's Inn Cookbook*

This recipe speaks eloquently of the culinary genius of Gary Hynes. We added ginger to the recipe without violating the spirit of the dish.

2 cups	buttermilk	500 mL
1	clove garlic, chopped	1
1 tbsp	ginger, grated	15 mL
1	onion, chopped	1
pinch of salt		
4	boneless chicken breasts	4
4	strips of bacon, cooked and crumbled	4
2 tbsp	butter	30 mL
1/2 cup	dry white wine	125 mL
4	dashes of apple cider vinegar	4
1 cup	chicken or soy stock	250 mL
4 tbsp	fresh, wild blueberries	60 mL
4	sage leaves, chopped	4
1/2 cup	butter	125 mL
4	sage leaves for garnish	4

꩜ Combine the first five ingredients in a large glass or ceramic bowl and marinate the chicken in this mixture overnight in the refrigerator.

꩜ Cook the bacon until crisp. Set aside.

꩜ Sauté the chicken breasts in 2 tbsp (30 mL) butter until done—do not overcook. (The chicken may also be grilled.)

꩜ Meanwhile make the sauce by combining the wine, vinegar, and stock in a saucepan and cook over high heat until the mixture thickens slightly. Add the blueberries, bacon, and chopped sage, then whisk in butter, a little at a time. Serve the sauce over chicken breasts. Garnish with sage leaves.

per serving
calories 581
g fat 45.4
g fibre 0.7

calorie breakdown
% protein 23
% fat 73
% carbohydrate 4

Serves 4

Lean Turkey Loaf

Adapted from Carol Ferguson and Margaret Fraser's *A Century of Canadian Home Cooking: 1900 Through the '90s*

The addition of finely chopped ginger to meat loaf immediately gives it gourmet interest.

6	green onions, chopped	6
1	clove garlic	1
2 tbsp	ginger, coarsely chopped	30 mL
1 cup	mushrooms, chopped	250 mL
1 tbsp	butter	15 mL
1 1/2 lbs	ground turkey or chicken	750 g
1 cup	fresh whole wheat bread crumbs	250 mL
1/2 cup	chopped parsley	125 mL
1 tsp	salt	5 mL
1/4 tsp	each, dried thyme and savory	1 mL
freshly ground black pepper to taste		

Sauté or microwave onions, garlic, ginger, and mushrooms in butter. Mix with turkey or chicken, bread crumbs, parsley, salt, thyme, savory, and pepper to taste.

Pack into a 9 x 5 inch (2 L) greased loaf pan and bake in preheated oven at 350°F (180°C) for about 1 hour.

Serve with Cranberry Ginger Relish (see page 13). This loaf is equally tasty served cold with a salad the next day.

Braised Duck in Soy Sauce

Adapted from Jim White's *Toronto Star Cookbook*

Transform a frozen supermarket duck into a tasty delicacy with this recipe.

1	duck (fresh or frozen), thawed, about 4 lbs (2 kg)	1
1 tbsp	vegetable oil	15 mL
2 1/2 cups	cold water	625 mL
1/2 cup	dark soy sauce	125 mL
2 tbsp	dry sherry	30 mL
4	green onions with tops, halved lengthways	4
3	slices ginger, each about 1/2 inch (1 cm) thick	3
2	whole pieces star anise	2
1/2	stick cinnamon	1/2
1/2 tsp	salt	2 mL
1 tbsp	toasted sesame oil	15 mL
1 tbsp	sugar	15 mL
lettuce leaves and tomato wedges for garnish		

Rinse duck, inside and out, and pat dry with paper towels. Trim and discard excess fat at base of tail and from inside cavity.

In a large saucepan or Dutch oven, heat oil over medium-high heat. Add duck and cook, turning, until it is brown all over. Stir in water, soy sauce, and sherry; add green onions, ginger, star anise, cinnamon, and salt. Bring to a boil, reduce heat and simmer, covered, 2 1/2 hours, or until brown and glazed. Turn the duck halfway through cooking period. Remove and transfer duck to heated serving platter lined with lettuce leaves. Reserve pan liquid.

Skim surface of the reserved liquid to remove excess fat; increase heat and reduce liquid to about 1 1/4 cups (300 mL). Stir in sesame oil and sugar. Pour sauce over duck. Garnish with tomato wedges.

	per serving
Serves 4	calories 382
	g fat 9.0
	g fibre 1.5
	calorie breakdown
	% protein 53
	% fat 21
	% carbohydrate 26

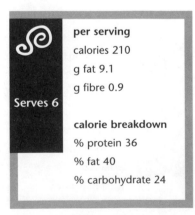

	per serving
Serves 6	calories 210
	g fat 9.1
	g fibre 0.9
	calorie breakdown
	% protein 36
	% fat 40
	% carbohydrate 24

Pork Roast with Rum

A popular dish from Caribbean cuisine, this one is guaranteed to warm the cockles of your heart in the dead of winter.

1	centre-cut pork loin roast with bone, about 5 lbs (2.5 kg)	1
4	cloves garlic, cut into slivers	4
1 tbsp	ginger cut in 1/2-inch (1 cm) slivers	15 mL
20	whole cloves	20
2 tsp	salt	10 mL
1 tsp	freshly ground black pepper	5 mL
1/2 cup	dark rum	125 mL
1 cup	brown sugar	250 mL
1 tbsp	ginger, grated	15 mL
2 tsp	garlic, finely chopped	10 mL
2 cups	chicken stock	500 mL
juice and zest of 2 large limes		
1 tbsp	cornstarch	15 mL
1/4 cup	water	50 mL

🍥 Poke holes over the surface of the meat with the tip of a sharp knife. Insert 2 or 3 garlic and ginger slivers in each hole, and poke the cloves into the meat at evenly spaced intervals. Rub meat all over with salt and pepper. Roast on a rack in preheated oven at 450°F (220°C) for 30 minutes. Reduce heat to 325°F (170°C) and roast for another 30 minutes.

🍥 Meanwhile, blend 2 tbsp (30 mL) of the rum with the brown sugar, ginger, and garlic.

🍥 After 1 hour, remove pork from oven. Pour stock into the roasting pan to deglaze it, and leave the stock in the pan. Rub pork with the brown sugar mixture and return it to the oven for 30 to 45 minutes. When the roast is done, remove from oven and let it rest while sauce is prepared.

🍥 Pour the liquid from the bottom of the roasting pan into a saucepan. Warm the remaining rum in a small skillet. Remove from heat and ignite it. Tilt the skillet back and forth until the flame goes out and add the rum to the liquid in the saucepan. Add lime juice and zest. Bring the sauce to a boil, and add the dissolved cornstarch in water mixture. Stir and cook the sauce until it thickens, and adjust the seasonings to taste.

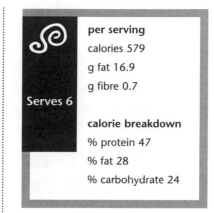

	per serving
🍥	calories 579
	g fat 16.9
	g fibre 0.7
Serves 6	
	calorie breakdown
	% protein 47
	% fat 28
	% carbohydrate 24

🍥 Slice the pork and arrange slices on a platter. Serve with rice and the sauce on the side.

Real Ginger Beef

Adapted from Craig Claiborne and Virginia Lee's *The Chinese Cookbook*

This is the best ginger beef recipe in the world. What else can we say?

1 lb	flank steak, sliced as thinly as possible across the grain	500 g
1 tbsp	cornstarch	15 mL
1 tbsp	soy sauce	15 mL
1 tbsp	toasted sesame oil	15 mL
1/2 tsp	freshly ground white pepper	2 mL
1 cup	ginger, finely shredded	250 mL
1 1/2 tsp	salt	7 mL
1 tsp	sugar	5 mL
3 tbsp	Shao hsing or dry sherry	45 mL
1 cup	peanut or vegetable oil	250 mL
2 cups	fresh coriander leaves, lightly chopped and firmly packed	500 mL

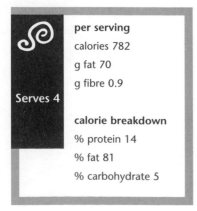

per serving
calories 782
g fat 70
g fibre 0.9

Serves 4

calorie breakdown
% protein 14
% fat 81
% carbohydrate 5

🍃 Marinate the beef in the cornstarch, soy sauce, sesame oil, and pepper for 30 minutes in refrigerator.

🍃 In a small bowl, toss the ginger with the salt and set aside for 20 minutes; then squeeze the shreds to extract most of their moisture, and set aside.

🍃 Combine the sugar and wine or sherry and set aside.

🍃 When the beef has marinated, heat the oil in a wok or skillet to a warm-hot temperature. Add the meat, stirring to separate the pieces. When the pieces change colour remove them to a colander to drain. (Do not overcook.)

🍃 Remove all but 3 tbsp (45 mL) of oil from the pan; heat the remaining oil and add the ginger. Stir rapidly for 15 seconds, add the beef, and cook, stirring for another 15 seconds. Stir in the coriander and wine mixture, and cook until just heated through. Serve with rice or angel hair pasta.

Baked Pumpkin with Beef and Ginger

Adapted from Time-Life Books Inc. *Foods of the World: Recipes: The Cooking of Latin America.*

Known in Latin America as carbonada criolla, *this spectacular dish has been the centrepiece of Margaret's Thanksgiving table for more than two decades. Easier than the traditional turkey to prepare, it never fails to elicit a recipe request. Peaches, corn, beef, and of course, the pumpkin, are essential, although Margaret's version has been known to have broccoli, parsnips, cauliflower, and a variety of summer and winter squashes. For real festive flair, bake and serve in six small, individual serving size pumpkins.*

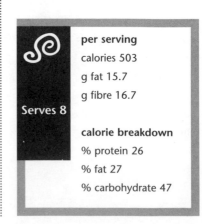

per serving
calories 503
g fat 15.7
g fibre 16.7

Serves 8

calorie breakdown
% protein 26
% fat 27
% carbohydrate 47

1	pumpkin, 10 lbs (5 kg)	1	
3 tbsp	butter	45 mL	
1/2 cup	sugar	125 mL	
2 tbsp	olive oil	30 mL	
2 lbs	sirloin tip, cut into 1-inch (2.5 cm) cubes	1 kg	
1 cup	onions, coarsely chopped	250 mL	
1/2 cup	green pepper, coarsely chopped	125 mL	
1 tsp	garlic, finely chopped	5 mL	
1 tbsp	ginger, finely chopped	15 mL	
4 cups	beef stock	1 L	
1 cup	tomatoes, peeled and chopped	250 mL	
1 tsp	dried oregano	5 mL	
1	bay leaf	1	
1 tsp	salt	5 mL	
freshly ground black pepper to taste			
1 1/2 cups	sweet potatoes, peeled and cut into 1-inch (2.5 cm) cubes	375 mL	
1/2 lb	white potatoes, peeled and cut into 1-inch (2.5 cm) cubes	250 g	
1/2 lb	zucchini, cut into 1/2-inch (2.5 cm) slices	250 g	
3	ears of corn, shucked and cut into 1 1/2-inch (3 cm) rounds or 1 (16-oz/ 500 mL) can of cob corn	3	
6	fresh peaches, peeled, halved and pitted or 1 (19-oz/ 540 mL) can peach halves, drained and rinsed in cold water	6	

❧ Scrub the outside of the pumpkin under cold running water with a stiff brush. With a large, sharp knife, cut into the top of the pumpkin to create a lid 6 inches (15 cm) in diameter. Leave the stem intact as a handle. Lift out the lid and, with a large metal spoon, scrape the seeds and stringy fibres from the lid and the pumpkin shell.

❧ Brush the inside of the pumpkin with soft butter and sprinkle the sugar into the opening. Tip the pumpkin from side to side to make the sugar adhere to the butter. Put the lid back in place.

❧ Place the pumpkin in a large shallow roasting pan and bake in preheated oven at 375°F (190°C) for 45 minutes, or until tender but somewhat resistant when pierced on the top with a sharp knife. The pumpkin shell must retain its form enough to hold the filling without danger of collapsing, so err on the side of caution.

❧ While the pumpkin is baking, heat oil over moderate heat in a large saucepan until a light haze forms over it. Add the cubes of meat and brown them on all sides, turning them frequently with a large spoon.

Regulate the heat so that the meat browns quickly without burning. Then with a slotted spoon, transfer the meat to a platter.

❧ To the fat remaining in the pan, add the onion, green pepper, garlic, and ginger. Cook over moderate heat, stirring constantly, for about 5 minutes, or until the vegetables are soft but not brown. Pour in the beef stock and bring to a boil over high heat. Return the meat and any of its accumulated juices to the pan and stir in the tomatoes, oregano, bay leaf, salt, and black pepper to taste. Cover the pan, reduce the heat to low, and simmer undisturbed for 15 minutes. Then add the sweet potatoes and white potatoes, cover the pan, and cook for 15 minutes; add the zucchini slices and corn rounds, cover the pan and cook for another 5 minutes. Finally, add the peaches and cook, covered, for another 5 minutes.

❧ Pour the entire contents of the pan carefully into the baked pumpkin, cover the pumpkin with its lid, and bake for another 15 minutes in preheated oven at 375°F (190°C). To serve, place the pumpkin on a large serving platter and at the table ladle the carbonada from the pumpkin onto heated, individual serving plates. Crusty bread is a must to sop up the tasty broth.

Heather's Lamb Stew with Doughboys

This is an exciting twist on Nova Scotia's traditional lamb stew with potatoes and doughboys: chickpeas, raisins, and ginger from its Middle Eastern cousin. Loosen your belts in advance of a carbohydrate overdose and a temporarily expanded waistline that you wont' regret!

Stew

1/4 cup	canola oil	50 mL
2 lbs	lamb stew pieces, ribs and lean pieces	1 kg
2 cups	chicken stock	500 mL
water to cover		
3 tbsp	ginger, chopped	45 mL
2	onions, chopped	2
3 tbsp	lemon juice	45 mL
1 cup	chickpeas, soaked over night	250 mL
1	turnip, cut in slices	1
6	carrots, cut in chunks	6
10	small onions, whole	10
3	leeks, chopped	3
6	potatoes, chopped	6
1/2 cup	raisins	125 mL
4	parsnips, chopped	4
freshly ground black pepper to taste		

Doughboys

2 cups	flour	500 mL
4 tsp	baking powder	20 mL
1/2 tsp	salt	2 mL
2 tbsp	shortening	30 mL
1 tbsp	chopped fresh parsley or coriander	15 mL
1 cup	milk	250 mL

Heat oil until a haze forms and brown lamb pieces. Remove with a slotted spoon to a separate dish. Drain off the remaining fat but leave the browning on the bottom of the pot.

Return meat to pot and add water and stock to cover. Add ginger, chopped onions, lemon juice, and chickpeas, and simmer for 1 hour. Remove some of the meat and add turnip, carrots, whole onions, leeks, potatoes, and raisins.

Place removed meat to top of the stew. Cook until nearly done. Add parsnips. Cook for 10 minutes more. Serve with doughboys.

In a bowl, mix flour, baking powder, and salt. Add shortening chopped into pea-size pieces. With fingers or a fork work the shortening into the flour. Add parsley or coriander and milk, stirring until mixed. Drop tablespoons of the mixture into the boiling stew, cover, and cook for 15 minutes. Don't peek.

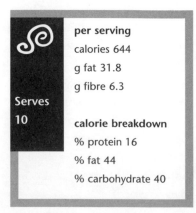

per serving
calories 644
g fat 31.8
g fibre 6.3

Serves 10

calorie breakdown
% protein 16
% fat 44
% carbohydrate 40

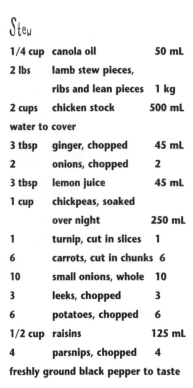

Moroccan Lamb Stew

Adapted from Sal Gilbertie's *Kitchen Herbs*

Lamb seems to have a special affinity for ginger. This rich stew needs only a salad—we suggest the Ginger, Grapefruit, and Avocado Salad on page 33—and a loaf of crusty bread. It's even better on the second day.

3 tbsp	olive oil	45 mL
1	large onion, thinly sliced	1
1 tbsp	ginger, chopped	15 mL
1 tsp	ground coriander	5 mL
3 1/2 lbs	boneless lamb, cut into 1-inch (2.5 cm) cubes	1.75 kg
1 cup	dried apricots	250 mL
12	large sprigs fresh coriander	12
2	bay leaves	2
1	sprig fresh thyme	1
3	cinnamon, sticks	3
2 tbsp	honey	30 mL
2 tbsp	lemon juice	30 mL
salt and freshly ground black pepper to taste		

In a heavy Dutch oven, heat olive oil. Add onion, ginger, and coriander. Sauté for 2 minutes. Add lamb and stir to coat with the onion mixture. Cover and cook over low heat for about 1 hour, adding a little water if necessary to prevent sticking.

Stir in apricots. Tie 6 sprigs of fresh coriander, bay leaves, thyme, and cinnamon with kitchen string. Place on top of meat; cover and simmer until apricots are tender, about 10 minutes.

Remove from heat and discard the coriander bouquet. With a slotted spoon, remove lamb and apricots to a heavy serving platter. Keep warm.

Stir honey into pan juices; boil to reduce and thicken the sauce. Stir in lemon juice and season with salt and pepper to taste. Pour the heated sauce over the lamb. Coarsely chop remaining fresh coriander and sprinkle over lamb.

per serving
calories 543
g fat 20.3
g fibre 0.6

Serves 6

calorie breakdown
% protein 38
% fat 34
% carbohydrate 28

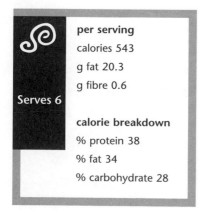

Gingerbread
& Cakes
Gingerbread
& Cakes
Gingerbread
& Cakes
Gingerbread
& Cakes

Parkin

A gingerbread that hails from Yorkshire and Lancashire, parkin is distinguished from its popular cousins by the coarse oatmeal (not rolled oats). It is baked in a shallow tin, kept in a piece, and served cut in squares. Allow it to "settle" for a day or two before eating, wrapped in foil to keep it moist. Traditionally spread with butter and eaten with cheese, parkin is a delicious afternoon tea accompaniment. We are indebted to Hilary Taylor for introducing us to the virtues of parkin.

1 cup	flour	250 mL
1/2 tsp	salt	2 mL
1 tsp	baking soda	5 mL
1 tsp	powdered ginger	5 mL
1/2 cup	medium oatmeal	125 mL
3/4 cup	soft brown sugar	175 mL
1/2 cup	butter	125 mL
1/2 cup	molasses or corn syrup	125 mL
1/2 cup	milk	125 mL
1/2 cup	mixed peel or chopped candied ginger	125 mL

✍ Sift the flour with the salt, baking soda, and ginger, and mix thoroughly with the oatmeal and sugar. Melt the butter with the molasses or corn syrup and add to dry ingredients with the milk. Stir in mixed peel or chopped candied ginger.

✍ Spread the batter in greased 8-inch (20 cm) square cake tin and bake in preheated oven at 350°F (180°C) for 50 minutes.

✍ After the parkin has cooled for 15 minutes, turn it onto a wire cooling rack. When completely cold, wrap in foil or store in an airtight container and leave for at least 1 day before cutting into squares for serving.

**Makes
12 large pieces**

per serving
calories 268
g fat 9.1
g fibre 0.4

calorie breakdown
% protein 4
% fat 30
% carbohydrate 66

Madame LeBlanc's Gingerbread

This recipe is from Josephine LeBlanc, Chéticamp, Cape Breton Island, a generous host and a great chef. Its use of tea or coffee is unusual, but invariably on hand in country kitchens.

1/2 cup	shortening or butter	125 mL
1 cup	molasses	250 mL
1	egg	1
2 cups	flour	500 mL
2 tsp	powdered ginger	10 mL
1/2 tsp	ground cloves	2 mL
2 tsp	baking soda	10 mL
1 cup	boiling water, tea, or coffee	250 mL

🌀 Beat the shortening or butter, add molasses and egg and mix well. Add the flour and spices and mix until blended.

🌀 Dissolve baking soda in boiling liquid and add to the batter. Stir carefully—it will be sloppy—until batter is smooth.

🌀 Pour into a 9-inch (22 cm) pan greased with butter or shortening and floured. Bake in preheated oven at 300°F (150°C) for 1 hour, or until it tests done.

🌀 Serve with Lemon or Butterscotch Sauce (page 81).

Variation: *Thinly slice 3 apples and spread on the bottom of the greased pan. Sprinkle 1/2 cup (125 mL) preserved ginger over the apple slices. Pour the batter carefully over the apples and ginger. When the cake is baked, leave in the pan for 10 minutes and turn out on a rack. Serve with whipped cream, or one of the ginger ice cream recipes (pages 103-105) or topped with a Lemon or Butterscotch Sauce (page 81).*

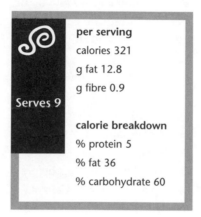

per serving
calories 321
g fat 12.8
g fibre 0.9

Serves 9

calorie breakdown
% protein 5
% fat 36
% carbohydrate 60

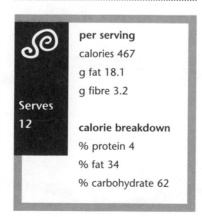

per serving
calories 467
g fat 18.1
g fibre 3.2

Serves 12

calorie breakdown
% protein 4
% fat 34
% carbohydrate 62

Marmalade Gingerbread

Adapted from Claire Macdonald of Macdonald's *Celebrations*

A stylistic variation of the classic makes this one a conversation stopper.

1 cup	milk	250 mL
2 tsp	baking soda	10 mL
1 cup	butter	250 mL
1 cup	marmalade	250 mL
1 cup	dark brown sugar	250 mL
2 1/2 cups flour		625 mL
1 1/2 tbsp ground ginger		22 mL
2 tsp	ground cinnamon	10 mL
2	large eggs, beaten	2
3/4 cup	raisins	175 mL
1/3 cup	preserved ginger, chopped	75 mL

🌀 Warm the milk and baking soda together and set aside.

🌀 Melt together the butter, marmalade, and brown sugar.

🌀 Sift together the flour, ground ginger, and cinnamon and mix into the melted butter mixture with the beaten eggs, mixing well. Stir in the warm milk and soda mixture, beating all together well. Stir in the raisins and chopped ginger.

🌀 Butter a 8 x 14 inch (20 x 30 cm) cake pan or loaf pan, and line the bottom with wax paper. Pour the mixture into the prepared pan and bake in preheated oven at 325°F (170°C) for 1 1/2 hours. Cool in the tin, cut into squares and serve with whipped cream.

Grandmother Stalker's Gingerbread Cake

This recipe, a legacy from Heather's grandmother, included lard, molasses, and boiling water, a winning combination—along with ginger—for a moist and tasty gingerbread.

1/2 cup	white sugar	125 mL
1/2 cup	shortening or butter	125 mL
1	egg	1
1 cup	dark molasses	250 mL
2 1/2 cups	all purpose flour	625 mL
1/2 cup	preserved ginger, finely chopped (optional)	125 mL
1 tsp	ground cinnamon	5 mL
1 tsp	ground ginger	5 mL
1/2 tsp	ground cloves	2 mL
1/2 tsp	salt	2 mL
1 1/2 tsp	baking soda	7 mL
1 cup	boiling water	250 mL
1 cup	blueberries, (fresh or frozen) (optional)	250 mL

In a mixing bowl, cream together the sugar, shortening or butter, egg, and molasses. In a separate bowl mix the flour, preserved ginger, cinnamon, ground ginger, cloves, and salt. Stir dry ingredients into creamed mixture. (The batter is quite thick.)

Dissolve baking soda in boiling water. Pour slowly into the batter. Mix the batter until it is smooth. Fold in the blueberries if using.

Pour immediately into a 10-inch (25 cm) square pan or an 8 x 14 inch (20 x 36 cm) pan that has been greased with butter and bottom lined with wax paper. Bake in preheated oven at 350°F (180°C) for 25 to 30 minutes, or until it tests done. Remove from the oven and let cake cool for 10 minutes before turning it onto a rack. Carefully remove the wax paper. Cut into squares and serve with whipped cream (try *Heather's variation), or ginger ice cream (pages 103-105), or topped with Lemon or Butterscotch Sauce (page 81).

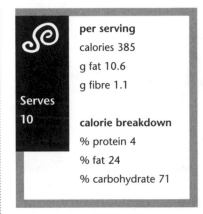

per serving
calories 385
g fat 10.6
g fibre 1.1

Serves 10

calorie breakdown
% protein 4
% fat 24
% carbohydrate 71

*Death by Ginger
Defying tradition, Heather adds 1/2 cup (125 mL) of finely chopped preserved ginger to her grandmother's already perfect recipe, and tops it with a cup of whipped cream laced with a spoonful of yogurt, 2 tsp (10 mL) of finely chopped preserved ginger, and 2 tbsp (30 mL) of ginger syrup (page 1).

Ancient Greeks used ginger as a digestive aid. After big meals, they ate ginger wrapped in bread. This medicinal practice evolved into our common "gingerbread."

Spiced Ginger Cake with Candied Ginger Cream

Adapted from Janet Hazen's *Turn it Up! 50 All-New Fiery Recipes* for *Cooking with Chilies, Peppercorns, Mustard, Horseradish, and Ginger*

This moist decadent cake is alive with the intense flavour of ginger in mass doses. Don't read the nutrient analysis if you are watching calories.

Cake

2 cups	sugar	500 mL
1 1/2 cups	vegetable oil	375 mL
4	eggs, lightly beaten	4
1 1/2 cups	carrots, finely grated	375 mL
1 1/2 cups	ginger, minced	375 mL
2 cups	all-purpose flour	500 mL
2 tsp	baking powder	10 mL
1 1/2 tsp	baking soda	7 mL
2 1/2 tbsp	ground ginger	35 mL
2 1/2 tsp	ground cinnamon	12 mL
2 1/2 tsp	ground mace	12 mL
1 1/2 cups	toasted walnuts, coarsely chopped	375 mL

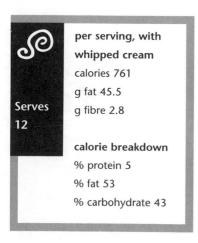

per serving, with whipped cream
calories 761
g fat 45.5
g fibre 2.8

Serves 12

calorie breakdown
% protein 5
% fat 53
% carbohydrate 43

In a large bowl, using an electric mixer, beat the sugar and vegetable oil together until pale and smooth, about 3 to 4 minutes. Add the eggs one at a time, beating well after each addition. Add the carrots and minced ginger and mix well.

Combine the flour, baking powder, soda, spices, and nuts, in a medium-size bowl; mix well. Add to the egg mixture and mix just until combined. Pour the batter into generously greased and floured 10 x 13 inch (25 x 33 cm) baking pan and bake on the lower rack of preheated oven at 350°F (180°C) for 30 minutes. Remove to the upper rack and bake for 20 to 25 minutes longer, or until it tests done. Remove from the oven and cool to room temperature. Run a dull knife around the edges of the cake before cutting.

Candied Ginger Cream

1 1/2 cups	whipping cream	375 mL
1/3 cup	icing sugar	75 mL
1 tbsp	ginger liqueur or light rum	15 mL
1 cup	candied ginger, finely chopped	250 mL

mint sprigs and sliced candied ginger for garnish

Place the whipping cream in a mixing bowl and using an electric mixer, beat on high speed until peaks form. Add the sugar and liqueur or rum and beat until firm enough to hold its shape but not stiff. Add the finely chopped candied ginger and mix gently.

Spread the top of each piece of cake with a generous dollop of the candied ginger cream and serve garnished with mint sprigs and candied ginger.

Ginger Pound Cake

Ginger adds character to this old standby, which keeps several weeks when stored in an airtight container or in the freezer.

4 cups	sifted cake flour	1000 mL
1 tsp	baking powder	5 mL
1 1/2 tsp	ground ginger	7 mL
1/4 tsp	mace	1 mL
1/4 tsp	salt	1 mL
2 cups	cold unsalted butter, cut into pieces	500 mL
1 tsp	freshly grated orange or lemon zest	5 mL
3 cups	sugar	750 mL
6	large eggs at room temperature	6
1/2 cup	packed minced ginger	125 mL
3/4 cup	milk at room temperature	175 mL

Into a bowl sift the flour with baking powder, ground ginger, mace, and salt. In a separate bowl, use an electric mixer to cream the butter with the zest at moderately high speed for 10 minutes, or until it is very high and fluffy, and add the sugar, 2 tbsp (30 mL) at a time, beating well after each addition.

Add the eggs, one at a time, beating after each addition. Add the minced ginger and beat the batter until it is well combined. Fold in flour mixture alternately with the milk, beginning and ending with the flour mixture, using 6 additions for the flour mixture and 5 for the milk and mixing the batter after each addition until it is just combined.

Pour the batter into a well buttered and floured 10-inch (25 cm) tube pan, 4 inches (10 cm) deep. Bake in the middle of a preheated oven at 300°F (150°C) for 1 hour and 45 minutes to 2 hours, or until it tests done.

Let the cake cool in the pan on a rack for 15 minutes and run a long, thin knife along the side. Invert the cake on a rack and let it cool completely.

In Elizabethan England, gingerbread men were called "gingerbread husbands."

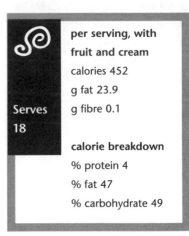

per serving, with fruit and cream
calories 452
g fat 23.9
g fibre 0.1

calorie breakdown
% protein 4
% fat 47
% carbohydrate 49

Serves 18

Serve this cake with fruit and whipped cream, a lemon glaze, or a drizzle of sherry.

Gingerbread Cream Pie
—George Washington

Adapted from *Kate Aitken's Cookbook*

Golden as a fall sunset,
Light as a fleecy cloud
Luscious as a sun-kissed berry—
That my friend is ...
Gingerbread Cream Pie—George Washington

Serves 8

per serving, with whipped cream
calories 615
g fat 15.6
g fibre 1.0

calorie breakdown
% protein 12
% fat 23
% carbohydrate 66

Cake

1/3 cup	butter	75 mL
1 cup	molasses	250 mL
1	egg	1
1 3/4 cups flour		425 mL
1/2 tsp	baking soda	2 mL
1 tsp	baking powder	5 mL
1/2 tsp	salt	2 mL
1 tsp	powdered ginger	5 mL
1 tsp	ground cinnamon	5 mL
1/4 tsp	ground cloves	1 mL
1/2 cup	milk	125 mL

✎ Cream together butter and molasses; add unbeaten egg and blend well. Add sifted dry ingredients alternately with milk. Beat until smooth.

✎ Pour batter into greased and floured round 9-inch (22 cm) cake pan. Bake in preheated oven at 350°F (180°C) until done, about 40 minutes.

✎ When cool, remove from pan and split in half. Put together with the following filling:

Filling

1 tbsp	gelatin	15 mL
1/4 cup	cold water	50 mL
1 cup	milk	250 mL
1 cup	sugar	250 mL
pinch of salt		
2 tbsp	cornstarch	30 mL
1	egg, well beaten	1
2 tbsp	dark rum	30 mL
1/2 cup	dried apricots or candied ginger, finely chopped	125 mL

✎ Soak gelatin in cold water for 10 minutes.

✎ Heat milk to scalding in top of a double boiler. In a small bowl, thoroughly mix together the sugar, salt, and cornstarch. Stir into hot milk, stirring constantly. Cook in top of double boiler until mixture begins to thicken.

✎ Add some of the hot milk mixture to the well-beaten egg and stir. Add the rum and apricots or candied ginger. Pour warm egg mixture into the milk

mixture. When slightly thickened, stir in gelatin until dissolved.

✎ Chill until mixture gels sufficiently to spread between layers of gingerbread.

Whipped Cream Topping

1 cup	whipping cream	250 mL
1 tbsp	sugar	15 mL
1/4 cup	candied ginger, finely chopped	50 mL

✎ Whip the cream until stiff; add sugar and candied ginger. Top filled cake with whipped cream mixture and serve.

Carrot Cake with Apricot Ginger Filling

Don't be put off by the low fat and calorie content of this cake—it's moist and flavourful all by itself. You can boost the calorie count—and the decadence—by serving it with ginger ice cream (see pages 103-105), or make it into a layer cake with Apricot Ginger Filling and topped with Cream Cheese Frosting.

1 1/2 tsp	baking soda	7 mL
1/4 cup	warm water	50 mL
1 1/2 cups	finely shredded carrots soaked in juice and zest of 1 lemon	375 mL
1/2 cup	plain non-fat or low-fat yogurt	125 mL
3/4 cup	brown sugar	175 mL
1/2 cup	drained crushed pineapple	125 mL
1/4 cup	canola oil	50 mL
1	egg (or 2 egg whites)	1
3 tbsp	ginger, grated	45 mL
2 tsp	ground cinnamon	10 mL
1/2 tsp	freshly grated nutmeg	2 mL
1/4 tsp	ground cloves	1 mL
1/4 tsp	allspice	1 mL
1/2 tsp	salt	2 mL
1 cup	currants	250 mL
1/2 cup	walnuts or pecans, chopped	125 mL
1/3 cup	fine unsweetened coconut	75 mL
1 1/4 cups	whole wheat flour	300 mL
1 1/4 cups	all-purpose flour	300 mL

In a small bowl, combine the baking soda and warm water. Set aside. In a large bowl, combine the soaked carrots, yogurt, sugar, pineapple, oil, egg or egg whites, ginger, spices, salt, currants, nuts, and coconut.

Stir in the flour followed by the baking soda mixture. Blend all the ingredients. Pour the batter into greased and floured 10-inch (25 cm) tube pan. Place the pan in preheated oven at 325°F (170°C) for 1 hour, or until it tests done.

Remove from the oven and let cake cool in its pan for 10 minutes before turning it onto a rack to cool completely. When cool, wrap in foil and serve the next day. The flavours blend with age.

Note: *For a layer cake, cut cake in two, and spread a mixture of thick, puréed Apricot Filling in the centre.*

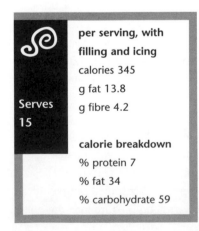

Serves 15	**per serving, with filling and icing**	
	calories 345	
	g fat 13.8	
	g fibre 4.2	
	calorie breakdown	
	% protein 7	
	% fat 34	
	% carbohydrate 59	

Apricot Ginger Filling

1 cup	organically grown apricots	250 mL
1/3 cup	chopped, preserved ginger	75 mL

Soak apricots in enough water to cover them. When softened, drain apricots and reserve 1/4 cup (50 mL) soaking water.

Purée the apricots and ginger with as much of the 1/4 cup (50 mL) of water as needed to make a thick paste.

Spread between layers of cake.

Cream Cheese Frosting

4 oz	cream cheese at room temperature	125 mL
	zest of 1 lemon	
1/4 cup	non-fat plain yogurt	50 mL
2 tbsp	icing sugar	30 mL
1/2 cup	whipping cream	125 mL

Cream the cheese and add the lemon zest, yogurt, and icing sugar. Blend well. Whip the cream and fold in the cream cheese mixture. Spread over cake just before serving.

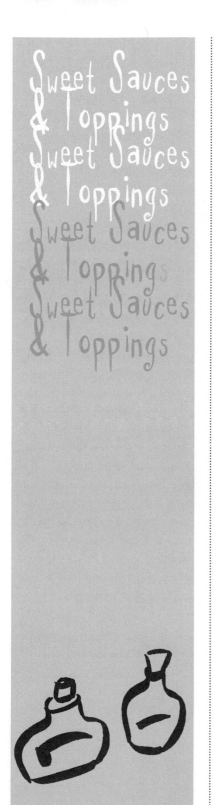

Lemon Sauce

This recipe from Margaret's mother, Gladys Slauenwhite, has stood the test of time. The tartness of citrus nicely complements the ginger in many of our cake recipes.

1/2 cup	sugar	125 mL
2 tbsp	cornstarch	30 mL
1 cup	water	250 mL
1/4 cup	lemon juice	50 mL
grated zest 1 lemon		
2 tbsp	butter	30 mL

🍥 In a small saucepan, mix together sugar, cornstarch, water, and lemon juice and zest. Bring to a boil over medium heat, stirring constantly until thickened and clear. Blend in butter.

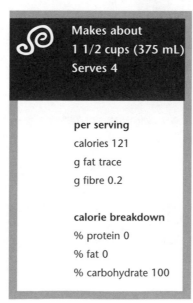

🍥 Makes about
1 1/2 cups (375 mL)
Serves 4

per serving
calories 121
g fat trace
g fibre 0.2

calorie breakdown
% protein 0
% fat 0
% carbohydrate 100

Butterscotch Sauce

Butterscotch Sauce and gingerbread is a traditional combination. We are indebted to Evelyn MacDonald for her popular household recipe.

2 tbsp	cornstarch	30 mL
1 cup	brown sugar	250 mL
2 cups	water	500 mL
2 tbsp	butter	30 mL
pinch of salt		

🍥 Mix the cornstarch and brown sugar in a saucepan.

🍥 Add the water and stir. Boil for 2 to 3 minutes. Sauce should be clear and brown.

🍥 Remove from heat and add butter and salt.

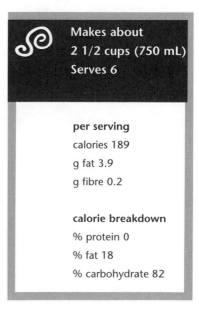

🍥 Makes about
2 1/2 cups (750 mL)
Serves 6

per serving
calories 189
g fat 3.9
g fibre 0.2

calorie breakdown
% protein 0
% fat 18
% carbohydrate 82

Caramel Ginger Sauce

Adapted from Eleanor Robertson Smith's *Loyalist Foods in Today's Recipes*

Delicious with vanilla ice cream, rice pudding, even cottage cheese, this sauce is another old-fashioned standby.

2 cups	sugar	500 mL
1 1/4 cups	hot water	300 mL
3 tbsp	candied ginger, chopped	45 mL

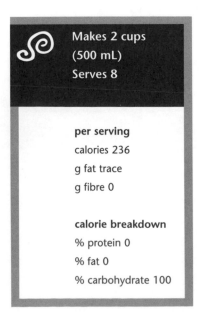 In a large saucepan, brown the sugar, stirring constantly over medium heat. Add hot water. Stir until smooth, about 4 minutes. Add ginger. Cool and serve. For a thicker sauce, boil (carefully) for another 4 to 5 minutes.

Makes 2 cups (500 mL)
Serves 8

per serving
calories 236
g fat trace
g fibre 0

calorie breakdown
% protein 0
% fat 0
% carbohydrate 100

Gingered Whipped Cream

This topping suits almost any dessert. Fold puréed fruit into this cream and dribble with chocolate sauce for a quick and easy dessert that guests will think took hours to make.

2 cups	whipping cream	500 mL
1 tbsp	sugar	15 mL
1/4 cup	preserved ginger, chopped	50 mL

 Whip the cream until it peaks, add sugar, whip briefly. Fold in ginger and serve.

Serves 8

per serving
calories 74.9
g fat 5.1
g fibre 0

calorie breakdown
% protein 2
% fat 59
% carbohydrate 39

Ginger Chocolate Sauce

This potent sauce embellishes just about anything—poached pears, angel food cake, ice cream—let your imagination run wild.

1/2 cup	cocoa powder	125 mL
1/2 cup	sugar	125 mL
1/2 tsp	powdered ginger	2 mL
3/4 cup	water	175 mL
1/4 cup	honey	50 mL
4 tbsp	preserved ginger, finely minced	60 mL
1 tsp	vanilla	5 mL

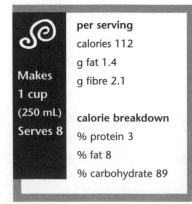 In a saucepan, combine the cocoa, sugar, and powdered ginger—make sure there are no lumps. Add water and stir.
  Bring to a boil over medium heat, reduce heat and add honey and preserved ginger. Boil gently until it thickens, about 10 to 15 minutes.
  Cool, then add vanilla. Pour into a jar and refrigerate.

Makes 1 cup (250 mL)
Serves 8

per serving
calories 112
g fat 1.4
g fibre 2.1

calorie breakdown
% protein 3
% fat 8
% carbohydrate 89

Cookies
Cookies
Cookies
Cookies
Cookies
Cookies
Cookies
Cookies

Butter Ginger Wedges

This delicious butter cookie (boterloek) was suggested to us by Heather's sister Joyce Pierce and contributed by Dutch Canadian Riet Vink, who sends "wedges" to relatives and friends at Christmas. It is a firm cookie, so it transports well and can be stored for a long time—perfect if you have gifts to send by mail.

1 cup	butter	250 mL
2 cups	all-purpose flour	500 mL
1 cup	sugar	250 mL
1	egg yolk	1
1/4 cup	preserved ginger, finely chopped	50 mL
1	egg white, slightly beaten	1

✿ Mix all ingredients except egg white in a bowl. Knead for final mixing.

✿ Press mixture in an 8-inch (20 cm) pie plate.

✿ Rub a slightly beaten egg white over the uncooked dough for a shiny glaze.

✿ Bake in preheated oven at 350°F (180°C) for 15 minutes. Remove from the oven and bang three times on a firm surface to make the batter fall. Bake another 15 minutes. Remove from the oven and repeat the banging.

✿ Mark the wedges. Cool and serve or store. Wedges will be a dense 3/4-inch (2 cm) thick cookie.

per slice
calories 207
g fat 11.2
g fibre 0.5

Makes 18 wedges

calorie breakdown
% protein 4
% fat 48
% carbohydrate 48

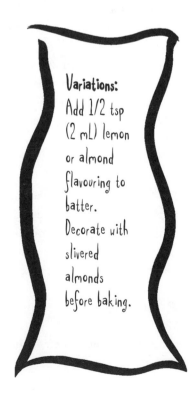

Variations:
Add 1/2 tsp (2 mL) lemon or almond flavouring to batter. Decorate with slivered almonds before baking.

Ginger Walnut Cookies

Susan McEachern got this recipe from a former student, Sheena Gourlay of Montreal. These cookies have become a Christmas tradition at Susan's house. They disappear quickly, so you may want to make two batches.

2/3 cup	butter	150 mL
2 cups	brown sugar	500 mL
2 tsp	baking soda	10 mL
4 tbsp	boiling water	60 mL
2 cups	flour	500 mL
2 tsp	vanilla	10 mL
1/2 cup	candied ginger, finely chopped	125 mL
1/2 cup	pecans or walnuts, chopped	125 mL

🌀 Cream the butter and brown sugar. Dissolve baking soda in boiling water and add flour. When well mixed add vanilla, ginger, and pecans or walnuts; stir until well distributed.

🌀 Form dough into small balls and place on a greased baking pan. Leave lots of room for them to spread. Press each ball down with a floured fork.

🌀 Bake in preheated oven at 325°F (160°C) for 10 to 15 minutes, watching carefully that they do not burn.

Gingersnaps

These cookies are a neighbourhood treasure for Dorothy Prokopiw, who writes: "My father's St. John's neighbour, Selma Tooton Perry, frequently delivers a tin of these wafer-thin, crispy snaps to his door." Well-spiced with ginger, these snaps are quite "moreish" with a cup of tea.

1 cup	butter	250 mL
1/2 cup	molasses	125 mL
2 cups	flour	500 mL
1/2 cup	white sugar	125 mL
1 tsp	baking soda	2 mL
5 tsp	ground ginger	25 mL

🌀 Mix softened butter and molasses.

🌀 Stir combined dry ingredients into molasses mixture and mix thoroughly.

🌀 Press dough in a wax-paper lined, small loaf pan, and freeze solid (about 4 hours in a freezer).

🌀 Gripping the wax paper, remove dough from the pan and then slice into thin rectangles. (Practice helps perfect this skill.)

🌀 Place on a lightly oiled cookie sheet. Bake in preheated oven at 375°F (190°C) until lightly browned. Depending on thinness, baking may only take 4 minutes. Check often to avoid burning.

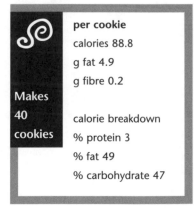

per cookie
calories 88.8
g fat 4.9
g fibre 0.2

Makes 40 cookies

calorie breakdown
% protein 3
% fat 49
% carbohydrate 47

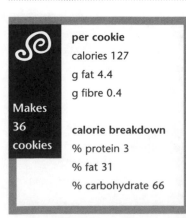

per cookie
calories 127
g fat 4.4
g fibre 0.4

Makes 36 cookies

calorie breakdown
% protein 3
% fat 31
% carbohydrate 66

Hot Gingersnaps

This is Heather's idea of a "hot" tea-dunking gingersnap.

1/2 cup	butter	125 mL
1 cup	molasses	250 mL
1/2 cup	brown sugar	125 mL
1 tbsp	vinegar	15 mL
3 cups	flour	750 mL
1 tsp	baking soda	5 mL
4 tbsp	ground ginger	60 mL
1 tsp	ground cinnamon	5 mL
1/2 tsp	grated nutmeg	2 mL
1/2 tsp	ground cloves	2 mL
pinch of salt		
1/4 cup	preserved ginger,	
	finely chopped	50 mL

✎ Bring the butter, molasses, brown sugar, and vinegar to a boil in a large saucepan. Stir to melt the butter. Cool to room temperature.

✎ Sift all the dry ingredients together. Add to the molasses mixture. Add the chopped ginger. Mix thoroughly and then knead.

✎ Divide the dough into 2 logs. Refrigerate until firm, about 1 hour.

✎ Slice the cookies thinly with a sharp knife, and bake on greased cookie sheets in preheated at 350°F (180°C) oven for 5 minutes.

✎ Cool and store in a container with a firm-fitting lid.

Fat Archies

Adapted from A Treasury of Nova Scotia Heirloom Recipes

Thick molasses cookies are often called "Fat Archies" on Cape Breton Island. Another even thicker version, called "Boulardarie Biscuits," is named after the area of Cape Breton where they were reputedly popular. A "substantial" cookie, Fat Archies are just the ticket with cheese and a mug of coffee.

2 1/2 cups flour		625 mL
1/2 tsp	ground cinnamon	2 mL
1 tsp	ground ginger	5 mL
1/2 tsp	freshly grated nutmeg	2 mL
1/2 cup	shortening	125 mL
1/2 cup	white sugar	125 mL
1/2 cup	brown sugar	125 mL
1	egg	1
1/2 cup	molasses	125 mL
2 tsp	baking soda	10 mL
1/2 cup	boiling water	125 mL
1 tsp	salt	5 mL

✎ Sift together flour, cinnamon, ginger, and nutmeg.

✎ Cream shortening. Add sugar and blend well. Add egg and mix. Then add molasses, and soda dissolved in boiling water. Add the sifted dry ingredients, mixing quickly to a smooth dough.

✎ Chill the dough. Roll out to 1/4-inch (1 cm) thickness and cut with a cookie cutter.

✎ Bake on greased cookie sheets in preheated oven at 400°F (200°C) for 15 to 20 minutes.

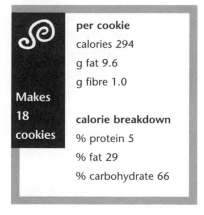

Makes 18 cookies

per cookie
calories 294
g fat 9.6
g fibre 1.0

calorie breakdown
% protein 5
% fat 29
% carbohydrate 66

Makes 60 cookies

per cookie
calories 64.5
g fat 1.7
g fibre 0.3

calorie breakdown
% protein 5
% fat 24
% carbohydrate 72

Mrs. Effie's Soft Molasses Cookies

When Margaret was growing up in Falkland Ridge, Nova Scotia, she lived "up the road" from Effie Sproule, who always seemed to have a pan of cookies baking in the oven. Children in the neighbourhood knew that they would have a treat if they hung around "Mrs. Effie's" kitchen long enough. Although they must have bored her silly, she never shooed them away without first offering a cookie, often a big, soft molasses cookie. Margaret's mother finally relented and asked Mrs. Effie for the recipe, which we now discover to our delight has a respectable quantity of powdered ginger in it. Mrs. Effie's molasses cookies are even more delectable if you throw in a half cup of finely diced preserved ginger!

1 cup	shortening	250 mL
1 cup	sugar	250 mL
1 cup	molasses	250 mL
4 tsp	baking soda	20 mL
1 cup	old-fashioned sour cream or buttermilk	250 mL
4 cups	all-purpose flour	1000 mL
2 tsp	ground ginger	10 mL
2 tsp	ground cinnamon	10 mL
1/2 tsp	ground cloves	2 mL
1/2 tsp	nutmeg	2 mL
1 tsp	salt	5 mL

Makes 24 cookies

per cookie, using cream/buttermilk
calories 250/236
g fat 11.0/9.2
g fibre 0.8/0.8

calorie breakdown
% protein 4/4
% fat 39/35
% carbohydrate 57/60

In a bowl, cream together shortening and sugar. Beat until light and fluffy. Add molasses. Dissolve baking soda in sour cream or buttermilk and add to the mixture, stirring well. Add sifted dry ingredients and blend into a soft dough.

Roll the dough out on a lightly floured board and cut rounds with a cookie cutter or the mouth of a 2 1/2-inch (6.5 cm) glass, powdered with a little flour to prevent sticking.

Bake on a greased cookie sheet in preheated oven at 350°F (180°C) for 12 to 15 minutes, or until they test done.

If these cookies last long enough to cool on a rack, you can decorate them with frosting for your guests, young and old.

Ginger Sparkles

This recipe came from Carolyn Bowlby, who worked as a secretary at Acadia University for over forty years. In the last decade of her career, she kept the history department sane with her periodic treats. Her scrumptious Ginger Sparkles have a healthy dollop of ginger, just right for this book.

3/4 cup	butter	175 mL
1 cup	brown sugar	250 mL
1/4 cup	molasses	50 mL
1	egg	1
2 cups	flour	500 mL
1 tsp	baking soda	5 mL
1/2 tsp	salt	2 mL
1 tsp	ground ginger	5 mL
1 tsp	ground cinnamon	5 mL
1/2 tsp	ground cloves	2 mL
granulated sugar for rolling		

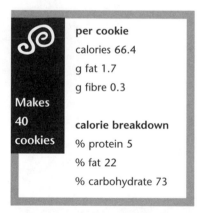

per cookie
calories 66.4
g fat 1.7
g fibre 0.3

Makes 40 cookies

calorie breakdown
% protein 5
% fat 22
% carbohydrate 73

Cream together butter, brown sugar, molasses, and egg until light and fluffy. Measure flour, soda, salt, and spices into a bowl. Stir into creamed mixture until blended.

Shape into small balls, 1 inch (2.5 cm) in diameter. Roll in granulated sugar and place 2 inches (5 cm) apart on a lightly greased baking sheet. Flatten with the back of a fork, dipped in milk.

Bake in preheated oven at 375°F (190°F) for 8 to 10 minutes. Cool slightly and remove from pan.

Gift—wrapped packages of ginger cookies leave lasting impressions!

Traditionally, in China at the birth of a child, a knob of ginger was tacked on the entryway of homes to absorb the negative character traits of any visitors.

Carrot Ginger Cookies

Margaret's mother found this recipe in a tattered old cookbook that has lost its cover and is so stained that it's difficult to read. Someone had the right idea early on for an easy, tasty, and healthy way to enjoy life.

2/3 cup	butter	160 mL
1 cup	honey	250 mL
2	eggs	2
1 cup	raisins	250 mL
1 cup	carrots, grated	250 mL
1/2 cup	preserved ginger, finely chopped	125 mL
1 3/4 cup	flour	425 mL
1/4 tsp	baking soda	1 mL
2 tsp	baking powder	10 mL
1/4 tsp	salt	1 mL
1/2 tsp	freshly grated nutmeg	2 mL
1/2 tsp	ground cinnamon	2 mL
2 cups	quick cooking oats	500 mL

✺ Cream butter and add the honey.

✺ Beat in eggs, one at a time. Stir in raisins, carrots, and ginger. Sift flour with baking soda, baking powder, salt, and spices; then stir into the mixture. Add oats and stir well.

✺ Drop by spoonfuls on a greased cookie sheet. Bake in preheated oven at 350°F (180°C) for 12 to 15 minutes.

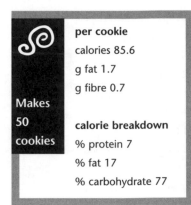

Makes 50 cookies

per cookie
calories 85.6
g fat 1.7
g fibre 0.7

calorie breakdown
% protein 7
% fat 17
% carbohydrate 77

The Greeks and Romans who bought their ginger from Arabian traders believed the line that it grew in the fabled land of the fish—eating Troglodytes, who were reputedly cave dwellers living on the edges of the earth.

Gingerbread Men and Women

No ginger cookbook would be complete without a recipe for gingerbread people. This tasty but sturdy dough is also great for gingerbread houses.

Gingerbread People

1/4 cup	butter	50 mL
1/2 cup	brown sugar	125 mL
1/2 cup	molasses	125 mL
1	egg	1
2 1/2 cups	flour	625 mL
1 tsp	baking soda	5 mL
1/2 tsp	ground cloves	2 mL
1 tsp	ground cardamom	5 mL
1 tsp	ground cinnamon	5 mL
1 tsp	ground ginger	5 mL
1/2 tsp	salt	2 mL

nuts, raisins, and preserved ginger for decoration

Icing

1/4 cup	icing sugar	50 mL

a few drops of water

Beat butter and sugar until creamy. Beat in molasses and egg.

Sift flour with baking soda, cloves, cardamom, cinnamon, ginger, and salt. Add the flour mixture. Mix and then knead until smooth. Chill dough for at least 1 hour.

Roll out the dough to desired thickness on a floured board.

Use cookie cutter to cut out the figures and carefully transfer them to greased baking sheets.

Bake on a greased cookie sheet in preheated oven at 350°F (180°C) for 8 to 10 minutes, according to the thickness.

Make icing by adding a few drops of water to icing sugar.

Apply the icing with a tooth-pick or a small knife for additional details, such as caps, hair, belts, and shoes.

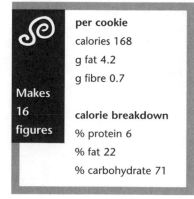

Decorate the gingerbread people with raisins, nuts, seeds, and bits of candied ginger before baking.

per cookie
calories 168
g fat 4.2
g fibre 0.7

Makes 16 figures

calorie breakdown
% protein 6
% fat 22
% carbohydrate 71

Desserts
Desserts
Desserts
Desserts
Desserts
Desserts
Desserts
Desserts

Rhubarb Fool with Ginger Cream

Adapted from Deborah Madison and Edward Espe Brown's
The Greens Cookbook

A fool—in the sense of cuisine—is an old English dessert made of custard and preserved fruit. This recipe is sensational, even with frozen rhubarb.

4 cups	rhubarb	1000 mL
1 cup	light brown sugar	250 mL
1/4 tsp	ground cloves	1 mL
1 tbsp	ginger, finely grated	15 mL
juice of 1/2 orange		
several large pieces of orange peel		
1 tsp	vanilla extract	5 mL
1 cup	whipping cream	250 mL
1 tbsp	sugar	15 mL
Grand Marnier to taste		
3 tbsp	preserved ginger, finely chopped	45 mL

Using young tender stalks, cut the rhubarb into 1-inch (2.5 cm) pieces, and put them in a saucepan with brown sugar, cloves, grated ginger, and orange juice and peel. Cook over medium heat until the rhubarb has melted into a thick purée and most of the water has cooked away, about 15 to 20 minutes. Stir toward the end of the cooking to make sure that the fruit does not scorch.

Once the rhubarb is cooked, add vanilla and transfer to another container. Cover and refrigerate.

When the fruit is cold, remove orange peel. Whip the cream with white sugar until it holds its shape. Add Grand Marnier and chopped ginger. Fold it into the rhubarb somewhat imperfectly to give it an irregular, marbled texture. Pile the mixture into tall glasses and serve. It will hold in the refrigerator several hours before serving.

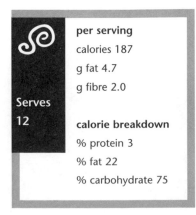

per serving
calories 187
g fat 4.7
g fibre 2.0

Serves 12

calorie breakdown
% protein 3
% fat 22
% carbohydrate 75

Mango Ginger Clouds

Adapted from *Ginger: A Book of Recipes*

This heavenly dessert is easy to make and low-fat. The secret to perfect "clouds" is ripe, juicy mangoes and high-quality silken tofu available in many health food stores.

3	ripe mangoes	3
3	1-inch (2.5 cm) pieces of stem ginger in syrup	3
3 tbsp	ginger syrup* or The King's Ginger Liqueur	45 mL
1/2 cup	silken tofu	125 mL
3	egg whites	3
6	pistachios, chopped	6

* See page 1

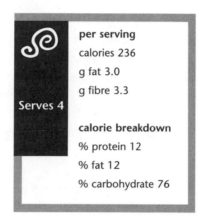

per serving
calories 236
g fat 3.0
g fibre 3.3

Serves 4

calorie breakdown
% protein 12
% fat 12
% carbohydrate 76

Note: Because of the potential for salmonella in the egg whites, do not serve this dish to children, pregnant women, or anyone who is ill.

Peel and roughly chop the mango flesh. Place in a blender or food processor with ginger, syrup, and tofu. Blend until smooth. Place in a bowl.

Put the egg whites into a bowl and whisk until they form soft peaks. Fold egg whites lightly into the mango mixture.

Spoon the mixture into wide dishes or glasses and chill well before serving, sprinkled with chopped pistachios.

Ginger Fruit Bowl

Adapted from *Just the Best: Favourite Recipes from Canada's Top Food Writers*

This recipe from Kate Bush produces the best fruit salad we have ever eaten. Margaret eats it every morning for breakfast and declares that she has never felt better.

1	cantaloupe, cut in chunks	1
1	pineapple, cut in wedges	1
2	pink grapefruit, peeled, seeded, & sectioned	2
2	mangoes, peeled & cubed or thinly sliced	2
1 cup	fresh blueberries or dried cherries or cranberries	250 mL
3 tbsp	ginger, grated	45 mL
2 tbsp	fresh lime juice	30 mL
2 tbsp	sugar	30 mL
2 tbsp	light rum or vodka, optional	30 mL

Combine ingredients in a glass serving bowl. Let stand for at least 30 minutes before serving.

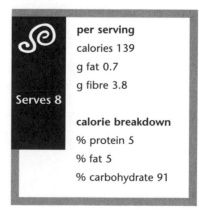

per serving
calories 139
g fat 0.7
g fibre 3.8

Serves 8

calorie breakdown
% protein 5
% fat 5
% carbohydrate 91

Ginger Baked Golden Delicious Apples

Adapted from *Jane Brody's Good Food Gourmet*

Baked apples, a staple in most Maritime households in the first half of the twentieth century, are now an overlooked delight. Versatile, easy to make, and very tasty, they can be eaten as an accompaniment to the main course or as dessert.

The secret of good baked apples, other than ginger, is the apple itself, which should be firm enough to hold together and soft enough to absorb the filling and melt in your mouth. At harvest time in the Annapolis Valley, there are at least twenty varieties of local apples to choose from, including Gravenstein, Cortlands, Pippins, Russets, and Kings. Experiment with the apples available to find which ones will work best. We found that the local Yellow Delicious had exceptional flavour. Fillings can range from chutneys and mincemeats to apricots and walnuts.

1/2 cup	dry white wine	125 mL
1/4 cup	apple cider or juice	50 mL
2 tbsp	sugar	30 mL
1 tbsp	butter	15 mL
2 tsp	ginger, grated	10 mL
1/8 tsp	ground cinnamon	0.5 mL
4	Golden Delicious apples	4
1/3 cup	golden raisins	75 mL

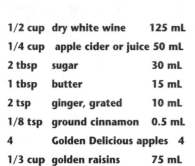 In a small saucepan, combine wine, cider or juice, sugar, butter, ginger, and cinnamon. Bring the mixture to a boil, stirring occasionally, and simmer for 5 minutes.

Core the apples. Peel top one-third of the apples, and place, peeled side up, in a baking dish. Fill the cavities with raisins and pour the wine mixture over the apples.

Place the uncovered dish in the middle of the oven.

Bake in a preheated oven at 350°F (180°C) for 30 minutes to 1 hour, or until the apples are tender but not mushy.

Serve warm, chilled, or at room temperature with the wine sauce poured over them.

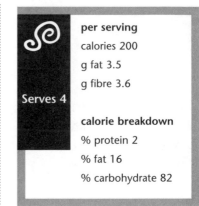

Serves 4

per serving
calories 200
g fat 3.5
g fibre 3.6

calorie breakdown
% protein 2
% fat 16
% carbohydrate 82

Variation: For a special occasion add a generous dollop of whipped cream, flavoured with 1 tsp (5 mL) sugar, 1 tbsp (15 mL) of ginger wine, and 1/4 cup (50 mL) of candied ginger.

Cider Baked Apples

Adapted from Bebe Ross Buszek's *The Apple Connection*

An inspiration to all of us, Bebe Ross Buszek would have approved of the "ginger connection" we explore.

4	firm apples	4
2 cups	apple cider or juice	500 mL
1/2 cup	brown sugar	125 mL
	grated zest of 1 lemon	
1 tbsp	ginger, grated	15 mL

✿ Core apples with an apple corer. Place them upright in a saucepan and add cider or juice until it reaches about halfway up the apples. Bring to a boil; then simmer gently, covered, until fruit is barely tender. Save the cider and remove apples to a serving dish.

✿ Add to the cider or juice 1/2 cup (125 mL) brown sugar, lemon zest, and ginger. Simmer until reduced to one cup.

✿ Remove from heat, cool and pour over apples. Serve with a pork roast or cold meat.

Variation: *Place the apples in an oven-proof pan, fill each apple cavity with Ginger Pear Chutney (page 10). Dot each apple with 1 tsp (5 mL) of butter and bake in preheated oven at 350°F (180°C) for 30 minutes to 1 hour, or until the apples are soft but not mushy. Serve warm with a roast of pork or lamb.*

Ginger Baked Granny Smiths

Adapted from Buderim Ginger Factory's *Little Ginger Cookbook*

4	Granny Smith apples	4
1/4 cup	chopped dried figs	50 mL
1 tbsp	butter, diced	15 mL
2 tbsp	ginger marmalade or preserved ginger	30 mL
1/2 tsp	ground cinnamon	2 mL
1/4 tsp	ground ginger	1 mL
1/2 cup	brown sugar, firmly packed	125 mL
1/4 cup	water	50 mL
1/4 cup	orange juice	50 mL
1/4 tsp	ground cinnamon	1 mL
1/4 tsp	ground ginger	1 mL
1/2 cup	sour cream	125 mL
	strawberries for garnish	

✿ Core apples, leaving a small amount of core at base. Slit the skins around the apples.

✿ Combine figs, butter, marmalade or preserved ginger, 1/2 tsp (2 mL) cinnamon, and 1/4 tsp (1 mL) ground ginger in a bowl. Press mixture into the centre of the apples.

✿ Place apples in an ovenproof dish and cook in preheated oven at 350°F (180°C) for 30 minutes.

✿ Stir brown sugar and water in saucepan over low heat until the sugar is dissolved. Stir in orange juice, 1/4 tsp (1 mL) cinnamon, and 1/4 tsp (1 mL) ginger.

✿ Pour sauce over partially baked apples and cook in a slow oven at 300°F (150°C) for another 30 minutes, or until apples are soft. Remove apples from dish and keep them warm.

✿ Transfer sauce to a small pan. Stir in sour cream. Simmer for 3 minutes.

✿ Serve apples whole or cut into quarters with sauce poured over them. Garnish with strawberries.

per serving
calories 257
g fat 0.5
g fibre 3.0

calorie breakdown
% protein 1
% fat 2
% carbohydrate 98

Serves 4

per serving
calories 324
g fat 9.0
g fibre 4.0

calorie breakdown
% protein 2
% fat 24
% carbohydrate 74

Blueberry Grunt

It is easy to guess how this traditional Maritime dessert got its prosaic name. When we added ginger, our guests grunted even louder with pleasure.

4 cups	wild blueberries	1000 mL
1/2 cup	sugar	125 mL
1/2 cup	water	125 mL
1 tsp	ground ginger	5 mL
2 cups	all-purpose flour	500 mL
4 tsp	baking powder	20 mL
1/2 tsp	salt	2 mL
2 tbsp	cold butter	30 mL
3 tbsp	preserved ginger, finely chopped	45 mL
3/4 cup	milk	175 mL

🌀 Boil blueberries, sugar, water and ground ginger in a large saucepan until juice is rendered, about 5 minutes.

🌀 Meanwhile, sift together flour, baking powder, and salt.

🌀 Cut in cold butter using a knife or your fingers. Stir in finely chopped ginger. Add sufficient milk to make a soft, sticky biscuit dough.

🌀 Drop by tablespoons in the hot berry mixture. Cover tightly and cook for 12 to 15 minutes. Serve with whipped cream.

Blueberry Buckle

This recipe comes from Judy McCluskey, who works at Mount Saint Vincent University. Judy suggests storing the leftover buckle in the refrigerator. In her house it mysteriously disappears before morning.

1/2 cup	shortening	125 mL
1 cup	sugar	250 mL
1	egg	1
	or 2 egg yolks	
2 cups	all-purpose flour	500 mL
1 tsp	ground ginger	5 mL
1 tsp	cinnamon	5 mL
1/2 tsp	salt	2 ml
1 cup	sour milk or buttermilk	250 mL
1 tsp	baking soda	5 mL
3 tbsp	molasses	45 mL
1 cup	blueberries	250 mL
3 tbsp	sugar	45 mL

🌀 Cream shortening and 1 cup (250 mL) sugar together. Add the egg or egg yolks and beat until light and creamy.

🌀 Sift together flour, ginger, cinnamon, and salt. Dissolve baking soda in sour milk or buttermilk. Add sifted dry ingredients to the creamed mixture alternately with sour milk or buttermilk mixture. Stir in the molasses; then fold in the blueberries.

🌀 Pour the batter into greased 9 x 9 inch (22 x 22 cm) cake pan. Sprinkle sugar over the batter in the pan and bake in preheated oven at 350°F (180°C) for 50 to 60 minutes.

🌀 Serve warm with Gingered Whipped Cream (page 82), ginger ice cream (pages 103–105), Lemon Sauce or Butterscotch Sauce (page 81).

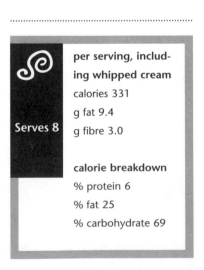

Serves 8

per serving, including whipped cream
calories 331
g fat 9.4
g fibre 3.0

calorie breakdown
% protein 6
% fat 25
% carbohydrate 69

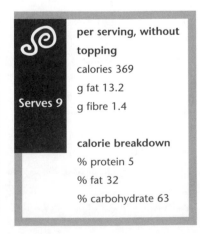

Serves 9

per serving, without topping
calories 369
g fat 13.2
g fibre 1.4

calorie breakdown
% protein 5
% fat 32
% carbohydrate 63

Ginger Crème Caramel

A basic formula for baked custard—2 cups (500 mL) of milk to 4 eggs—varies depending upon the fat content of the milk. For those trying to avoid cream, this recipe works well with 2% milk.

Custard

2 cups	2% milk or	
	half-and-half	500 mL
1/4 cup	sugar	50 mL
1 tbsp	ginger juice*	15 mL
2 tbsp	coconut cream	30 mL
4	eggs	4

* See page viii

Caramel

1/2 cup	sugar	125 mL
1 tbsp	chopped preserved ginger,	
	or more to taste	15 mL

🍥 In a double boiler, scald together the milk or half-and-half and sugar.

🍥 Add the ginger juice and coconut cream. Cover and set aside.

🍥 Beat the eggs and gradually add the milk mixture. Strain through a sieve.

🍥 Make the caramel by stirring and heating sugar in a saucepan until it has liquefied and turned golden brown. Remove immediately from heat and pour into casserole dish or individual custard cups. Work quickly. Sprinkle the chopped ginger over the caramel and pour in the custard mixture.

🍥 Set the dish or cups in a pan of hot water. Bake in preheated oven at 325°F (160°C) until a knife, inserted in the centre of one of the custards, comes out clean, about 40 minutes. Serve with whipped cream or more chopped crystallized ginger.

🍥 Serves 4

per serving
calories 354
g fat 12.0
g fibre 0.2

calorie breakdown
% protein 12
% fat 30
% carbohydrate 58

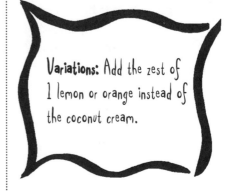

Variations: Add the zest of 1 lemon or orange instead of the coconut cream.

Maple Ginger Mousse

Adapted from Marie Nightingale's
Out of Old Nova Scotia Kitchens

Linda Cann produces this edible wonder every year for a table that groans at her January open house.

1 tbsp	gelatin	15 mL
1/4 cup	cold water	50 mL
2	eggs	2
1/2 cup	milk	125 mL
1 cup	maple syrup	250 mL
1 cup	heavy cream	250 mL
1/4 cup	reserved ginger, chopped	50 mL

✿ Soak the gelatin in the cold water.

✿ Beat the eggs and put into the top of a double boiler along with milk and maple syrup. Stir well, and cook until mixture thickens. Add gelatin mixture and stir until thoroughly dissolved. Set aside to cool.

✿ When the mousse begins to set, whip cream until stiff and combine with the mousse mixture. Then add the chopped ginger. Turn into a mould that has been dipped in cold water. You may prefer to use individual moulds. Chill until firm.

✿ Turn out on serving plate and garnish with whipped cream and diced candied ginger.

Ginger Trifle

Adapted from *Bermudian Cookery*

For fun we added chopped preserved ginger to this recipe, but it packs a punch without the additional ginger. Make this trifle the morning of the party and refrigerate it. We are indebted to Sheila Gosling for this conversation-stopping dessert.

4 cups	heavy whipping cream	1 L
1 tbsp	sugar	15 mL
1 tbsp	ginger, chopped	15 mL
1 cup	preserved ginger, chopped (optional)	250 mL
1 cup	sweetened shredded coconut	250 mL
1 cup	walnuts, chopped	250 mL
1/2 cup	sugar	125 mL
3/4 cup	Drambuie	175 mL
2 tbsp	Scotch	30 mL
1	box commercial gingersnaps	350 g
1/2 cup	chopped crystallized ginger for garnish	125 mL

✿ Whip cream until stiff and beat in 1 tbsp (15 mL) of sugar. Except for the gingersnaps, fold in the rest of the ingredients one at a time, ending with the Scotch. Mix well.

✿ Place a layer of gingersnaps in a large serving bowl, add a thick layer of whipped cream mixture, then another layer of gingersnaps, and so on, until the whipped cream mixture is exhausted, ending with a layer of whipped cream.

✿ Garnish with crystallized ginger and refrigerate until serving time.

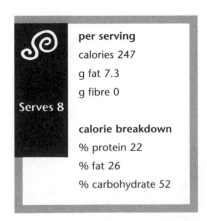

Serves 8

per serving
calories 247
g fat 7.3
g fibre 0

calorie breakdown
% protein 22
% fat 26
% carbohydrate 52

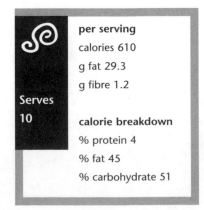

Serves 10

per serving
calories 610
g fat 29.3
g fibre 1.2

calorie breakdown
% protein 4
% fat 45
% carbohydrate 51

Baked Indian Pudding

Adapted from *A Treasury of Nova Scotia Heirloom Recipes*

Also called Stir Pudding, this recipe is attributed to the Loyalists who came to the Maritimes during and after the American Revolution (1776–1783). The name derives from the use of cornmeal, which was also known as Indian meal. This recipe yields a layered pudding with custard on the top and baked cornmeal on the bottom. For a more consistent texture, cook the soaked cornmeal in the scalded milk for about 10 minutes before baking.

1/4 cup	cornmeal	50 mL
1 cup	cold water	250 mL
2 cups	scalded milk	500 mL
1 1/2 tbsp	butter	22 mL
1/2 cup	brown sugar	125 mL
2	eggs, beaten	2
1/2 tsp	salt	2 mL
1/2 tsp	ground ginger (we doubled this amount)	2 mL
1/2 tsp	ground cinnamon	2 mL
1/2 cup	molasses	125 mL
1/4 cup	raisins (optional)	50 mL
1 cup	cold milk	250 mL

✆ Stir cornmeal into cold water. Add scalded milk, stir in remaining ingredients, except cold milk. Pour batter into buttered 2-qt (2 L) casserole. Pour cold milk over batter—do not stir!

✆ Bake in preheated oven at 300°F (150°C) for 2 1/2 hours.

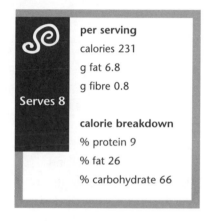

per serving
calories 231
g fat 6.8
g fibre 0.8

Serves 8

calorie breakdown
% protein 9
% fat 26
% carbohydrate 66

Variations: Traditionally this pudding was served with cream but it is also tasty with whipped cream, Butterscotch Sauce (page 81), or fresh fruit, such as raspberries or sliced peaches.

Ginger Cheesecake

Adapted from Anna Thomas' *The Vegetarian Epicure*

Since the early 1970s Anna Thomas' recipes have been an inspiration for our palates, like this recipe for ginger cheesecake, a must in every ginger-lover's repertoire. Anna Thomas calls for a pastry brisée crust, but we often substitute one made from graham crackers or gingersnaps.

Sweet Pastry

1 cup	all-purpose flour	250 mL
1/3 cup	sugar	75 mL
pinch of salt		
1/2 cup	butter	125 mL

 Sift together the flour, sugar, and salt. Cut in butter with a pastry blender until it has the texture of coarse sand. Continue working it with your hands until you can pat the dough into a ball. Refrigerate for 1 to 2 hours.

 Press pastry into a 10-inch (25 cm) pie pan until it is even and fairly smooth. Flute the edges, keeping them inside the pan. Prick the bottom with a fork for steam-escape holes. Put a layer of foil in the bottom of the crust and fill to about 1 inch (2.5 cm) with some dried beans.

 Bake in preheated oven at 450°F (230°C) for about 10 minutes.

Filling

1 3/4 cups	cream cheese	425 mL
1/2 cup	sugar	125 mL
2	eggs	2
2 tsp	lemon juice	10 mL
1 tbsp	ginger, grated	15 mL
1 1/2 cups	sour cream	375 mL
5 tbsp	sugar	75 mL
2 tbsp	crystallized ginger, slivered	30 mL

 In a mixing bowl, blend the cream cheese, sugar, eggs, lemon juice, and grated ginger. Beat until the mixture is very smooth and pour into baked pie shell.

 Bake in preheated oven at 350°F (180°C) for 25 to 30 minutes.

 Mix the sour cream with 5 tbsp (75 mL) sugar and the slivered ginger. Spread over the cheese filling while it is still hot from the oven. Turn the oven off, and return the pan for a few minutes, then remove and chill well in the refrigerator.

per serving
calories 289
g fat 19.9
g fibre 0.3

Serves 16

calorie breakdown
% protein 6
% fat 61
% carbohydrate 33

Ginger-Brandy Cheesecake

Adapted from Molly Katzen's *Moosewood Cookbook*

A Moosewood classic, this cheesecake makes the ideal dinner party dessert. With ginger in the crust, the filling, and the glaze, it's a real "hit."

Gingersnap Crust

5 tbsp	butter	75 mL
2 tbsp	honey	30 mL
2 cups	finely crumbled gingersnaps	500 mL

Melt butter and honey together. Add to gingersnap crumbs and mix well.

Press firmly onto the base of an assembled springform pan.

Filling

1 1/2 cups	cream cheese	375 mL
1 1/2 cups	sour cream	375 mL
4	large eggs	4
5 tbsp	honey	75 mL
2 tbsp	brandy	30 mL
1 tbsp	grated ginger	15 mL
dash of salt		

Whip all ingredients together with an electric beater.

Pour batter into the prepared crust and bake in a preheated oven at 350°F (180°C) for about 40 to 50 minutes, or until it test done.

Let cake cool completely before topping with the glaze.

Glaze

3/4 cup	orange juice	175 mL
2 tbsp	cornstarch	30 mL
2 tbsp	honey	30 mL
2 tsp	brandy	10 mL
1/4 tsp	orange zest	1 mL
strips of candied ginger		

Whisk orange juice and cornstarch in a small saucepan. Cook, whisking constantly, until thick and glossy, about 8 minutes. Remove from heat. Keep whisking and add remaining ingredients.

Pour over cooled cheesecake. Decorate with candied ginger.

Chill thoroughly for several hours before serving.

per serving
calories 320
g fat 19.0
g fibre 0.2

Serves 16

calorie breakdown
% protein 7
% fat 53
% carbohydrate 40

Mom's Pumpkin Pie

Margaret's mother makes the best pies in the world. Converted to more healthy eating later in life, she substituted reduced milk for cream, whole wheat for white flour, and reduced the amount of sugar—but her pies only improved.

Crust

3/4 cup	whole wheat flour	175 mL
3/4 cup	all-purpose flour	175 mL
1 tbsp	brown sugar	15 mL
1/2 cup	butter	125 mL
5 tbsp	water, to blend	75 mL

🌀 Mix together flours and sugar. Cut butter into flour mixture until it has the texture of coarse meal. Add only enough water to allow the dough to hold together to form a ball. Roll out on a floured board to 1/4 inch (0.5 cm) thickness and press into a 9-inch (22 cm) pie plate. Set aside.

Filling

1 1/2 cups	pumpkin purée	375 mL
2 tbsp	flour	30 mL
1/2 cup	brown sugar	125 mL
3 tbsp	ginger, grated	45 mL
1/2 tsp	ground cinnamon	2 mL
1/4 tsp	ground cloves	1 mL
1/4 tsp	allspice	1 mL
1/4 tsp	ground nutmeg	1 mL
1/4 tsp	salt	1 mL
2	eggs	2
1 cup	cream or whole or canned milk	250 mL

🌀 Mix together pumpkin, flour, sugar, all the spices, and salt.

🌀 Beat eggs into the cream or milk and add to pumpkin mixture.

🌀 Pour into pie shell and bake in preheated oven at 425°F (220°C) for 15 minutes. Reduce heat to 350°F (180°C) and bake for 30 minutes, or until it tests done.

🌀 Serve with a dollop of whipped cream, sweetened with 1 tsp (5 mL) of white sugar and 1 tsp (5 mL) of almond flavouring.

Serves 8

per serving, with whipped cream
calories 397
g fat 19.8
g fibre 2.0

calorie breakdown
% protein 6
% fat 44
% carbohydrate 50

Ginger Walnut Tart

A winner at any dinner party, this tart is intense with flavour. Serve it with ginger ice cream (pages 103-105) and drizzled with chocolate when you want to make a lasting impression.

Pastry

1 1/4 cups all-purpose flour 300 mL
1/2 cup   cold unsalted butter,
**   cut into bits   125 mL**
1/4 tsp   salt   1 mL
1 tsp   white vinegar   5 mL
3 tbsp   ice water   45 mL

In a large bowl, blend flour, butter, and salt until the mixture resembles meal. Mix vinegar and ice water and add to flour mixture. Toss until the liquid is incorporated, and form the dough into a ball.

Knead the dough lightly with the heel of the hand against a smooth surface for a few seconds to distribute the fat evenly and re-form into a ball.

Dust the dough with flour and chill it, wrapped in wax paper, for 1 hour.

Filling

1 3/4 cups light brown
**   sugar   425 mL**
1/2 cup   loosely packed, finely
**   chopped ginger   125 mL**
4   large eggs,
**   lightly beaten   4**
2 tbsp   heavy cream   30 mL
1 tsp   vanilla   5 mL
1/4 tsp   salt   1 mL
1/3 cup   unsalted butter,
**   melted   75 mL**
1 1/2 cups coarsely chopped
**   walnuts   375 mL**

To prepare the pastry shell: Roll the dough 1/8 inch (3 mm) thick on a lightly floured surface and fit into a 9-inch (22 cm) tarte pan with a removable fluted rim. Trim the edge, leaving 1/2-inch (1.5 cm) overhang; fold the overhang inward onto the side of the shell, pressing it firmly to extend the height of the rim by 1/4 inch (1 cm). Chill shell for one hour.

In a bowl, combine well the brown sugar, ginger, eggs, cream, vanilla, and salt; add the butter in a stream, whisking until the mixture is well combined.

Sprinkle the walnuts over the bottom of the shell, pour the mixture into the shell, and bake the tart in the middle of a preheated oven at 325°F (160°C) for 1 hour, or until the filling is puffed and just set.

Let the tart cool completely in the pan on a rack and serve it with ice cream or whipped cream.

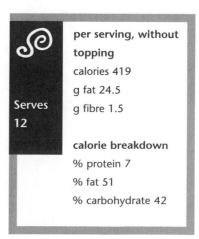

per serving, without topping
calories 419
g fat 24.5
g fibre 1.5

Serves 12

calorie breakdown
% protein 7
% fat 51
% carbohydrate 42

Pear and Ginger Tart

Adapted from Janice Poon and Dinah Koo's *Dinah's Cupboard Cookbook*

This recipe is a favourite of our publisher Dorothy Blythe and has become a favourite of ours, too. Life is too short to make puff pastry. Buy it ready-made.

Crème Fraîche

1 cup	sour cream	250 mL
1 cup	whipping cream	250 mL

Tart

1/2 lb	puff pastry	250 mL
1/3 cup	butter	75 mL
3/4 cup	sugar	175 mL
1 tbsp	ginger, finely shredded	15 mL
2 tsp	lemon zest, finely shredded	10 mL
1 tbsp	lemon juice	15 mL
5	Bosc pears, peeled, cored, and quartered	5

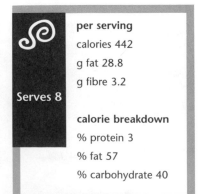

per serving
calories 442
g fat 28.8
g fibre 3.2

Serves 8

calorie breakdown
% protein 3
% fat 57
% carbohydrate 40

To make crème fraîche, whisk together sour cream and whipping cream in a medium-size bowl. Cover with plastic wrap and let stand in a warm place overnight or until thickened.

For tart, roll the pastry dough 1/8 inch (3 mm) thick on a lightly floured surface. Cut out a 12-inch (30 cm) circle. Prick all over with a fork and refrigerate.

In a heavy 10-inch (25 cm) saucepan with ovenproof handle, melt butter and sugar together over medium heat until sugar starts to turn light brown. Add ginger, lemon zest, lemon juice, and pears and cook, turning occasionally, until the sugar has caramelized and the pears have softened, about 15 minutes.

Top with pastry. Bake for 15 minutes or until pastry is golden brown. Invert onto a platter and present pear side up. Serve warm topped with crème fraîche.

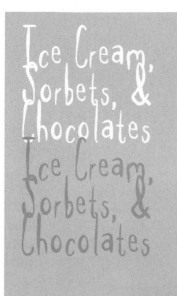

Ice Cream,
Sorbets, &
Chocolates

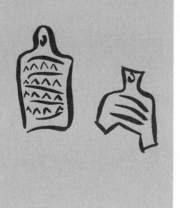

Ginger Yogurt Ice Cream

Ginger ice cream, one of the staples of our freezers, is a treat on its own, with ginger or maple syrup, gingerbread, fruit salad, or pie. We offer three recipes, all delicious.

2 cups	light cream (10 %)	500 mL
2 cups	low-fat yogurt	500 mL
1 cup	sugar	250 mL
dash of salt		
2 cups	whipping cream	500 mL
1 tbsp	pure vanilla extract	15 mL
1 cup	preserved ginger, coarsely chopped	250 mL

Combine all ingredients. Cover and refrigerate for 30 minutes, then freeze according to ice cream maker instructions.

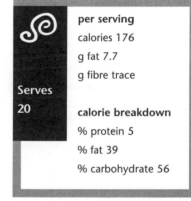

per serving
calories 176
g fat 7.7
g fibre trace

Serves
20

calorie breakdown
% protein 5
% fat 39
% carbohydrate 56

In season, add 1 cup (250 mL) of crushed fresh strawberries or peaches for a truly divine eating experience.

Satin Ginger Ice Cream

This recipe makes the most decadent ginger ice cream we have ever tasted. To avoid raising your cholesterol count beyond an acceptable limit, consume in small doses.

1 cup	water	250 mL
1/2 cup	sugar	125 mL
1/2 cup	coarsely chopped ginger	125 mL
6	egg yolks	6
3/4 cup	honey	175 mL
2 cups	coffee cream (18%)	500 mL
2 cups	whipping cream	500 mL

Place water, sugar, and ginger in a small saucepan and simmer for 15 to 20 minutes. Let cool completely. Pass through a strainer to remove the chopped ginger.

In the top of a double boiler, whisk the egg yolks. Add the honey, coffee cream, and cooled ginger syrup. Cook over simmering water, stirring frequently, until the mixture thickens slightly, about 15 minutes. Cool and then refrigerate until chilled.

Remove the egg mixture from the refrigerator and stir in the whipped cream. Freeze according to ice cream maker instructions.

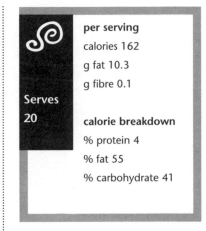

per serving
calories 162
g fat 10.3
g fibre 0.1

Serves 20

calorie breakdown
% protein 4
% fat 55
% carbohydrate 41

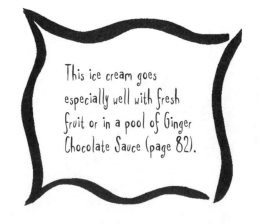

This ice cream goes especially well with fresh fruit or in a pool of Ginger Chocolate Sauce (page 82).

Old-Fashioned Ginger Ice Cream

Creamy-delicious—this ice cream is even better than we remember it as children!

1 cup	sugar	250 mL
3 tbsp	flour	45 mL
1/4 tsp	salt	1 mL
3 cups	light cream (10%)	750 mL
2	eggs, beaten	2
2 cups	whipping cream	500 mL
1 tsp	pure vanilla extract	5 mL
1 cup	preserved ginger, coarsely chopped, with at least 3 tbsp (45 mL) of the syrup it is preserved in or ginger syrup*	250 mL

*See page 1

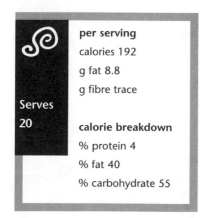

per serving
calories 192
g fat 8.8
g fibre trace

Serves 20

calorie breakdown
% protein 4
% fat 40
% carbohydrate 55

Combine sugar, flour, and salt in saucepan. Gradually stir in light cream. Cook over medium heat for about 15 minutes, or until thickened, stirring constantly.

Gradually stir about 1 cup (250 mL) of the hot cream mixture into the beaten eggs. Add the remaining hot mixture, stirring constantly. Cook 1 minute and remove from heat.

Refrigerate for two hours. Combine the whipping cream, vanilla, preserved ginger and syrup in a large bowl. Add the chilled mixture, stirring with a wire whisk to combine. Freeze according to ice-cream maker instructions.

To serve, allow this rich ice cream to soften slightly so that its creaminess can be best experienced.

Apple, Ginger, and Mint Sorbet

Adapted from Janet Hazen's *Turn it Up! 50 All-New Fiery Recipes for Cooking with Chilies, Peppercorns, Mustard, Horseradish, and Ginger*

This sorbet can be served as a palate cleanser or as a light—but memorable—dessert.

3 cups	water	750 mL
3 cups	sugar	750 mL
1/2 cup	ginger, coarsely chopped, firmly packed	125 mL
1 cup	fresh mint leaves, coarsely chopped, firmly packed	250 mL
2	large tart green apples, peeled, cored, and finely chopped	2
1/3 cup	lemon juice	75 mL
3 tbsp	ginger, finely chopped	45 mL
20	ice cubes, coarsely chopped	20
mint sprigs for garnish		

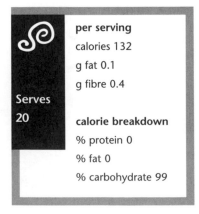

per serving
calories 132
g fat 0.1
g fibre 0.4

Serves 20

calorie breakdown
% protein 0
% fat 0
% carbohydrate 99

🍥 In a large, heavy-bottom saucepan, combine the water, sugar, coarsely chopped ginger, and 1 cup (250 mL) chopped mint. Bring to a boil over high heat, stirring constantly. Boil for 35 to 40 minutes, stirring frequently to prevent the mixture from boiling over, until mixture is thick and syrupy.

🍥 Remove from heat and strain through a fine wire sieve.

🍥 Return the syrup to the saucepan and bring to a boil over high heat; cook 3 minutes, stirring constantly. Add the apples and lemon juice and cook for 3 or 4 minutes, or until the apples are just tender.

🍥 Remove from the heat and cool slightly. Add the 3 tbsp (45 mL) finely chopped ginger and mix well.

🍥 In a blender, purée the mixture until smooth, stopping occasionally to scrape the sides of the container. Transfer to a non-reactive container and freeze for at least 6 hours, or up to 2 days. (The mixture won't freeze solid, but it will become slushy.)

🍥 Before serving, place half the ice cubes and half the fruit mixture in a blender. Blend until the ice is finely crushed and the mixture is smooth and icy. If you are serving only 3 or 4 people, stop at this point and reserve the other half for later use. Otherwise, blend the remaining ice cubes and fruit mixture. Serve immediately, garnished with sprigs of fresh mint.

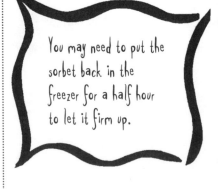

You may need to put the sorbet back in the freezer for a half hour to let it firm up.

Blueberry Ginger Sorbet

Once we started testing recipes on our friends, they began to do research for us. This refreshing sorbet, best with wild Nova Scotia berries, is from Gwen Davies.

1 cup + 2 tbsp	sugar	280 mL
1 cup + 2 tbsp	water	280 mL
3 tbsp	ginger, grated	45 mL
6 cups	wild blueberries	1.5 L
1/4 cup	lemon juice	50 mL

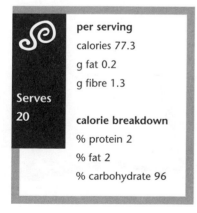 Combine the sugar, water, and ginger in a medium saucepan and bring to a boil. Reduce heat and simmer for 5 minutes. Let stand until cool.

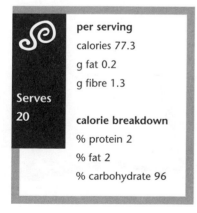 Place the blueberries, ginger syrup, and lemon juice in a blender and blend until smooth. Strain through a fine wire sieve.

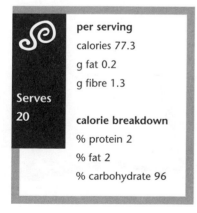 Refrigerate until cold. Freeze according to directions in an ice-cream maker.

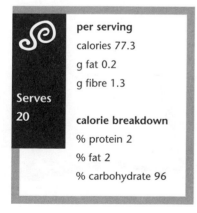 Before serving, take the sorbet out of the freezer and let stand for a half hour. The flavours of the blueberries, ginger, and lemon are best when the sorbet is softened slightly.

per serving
calories 77.3
g fat 0.2
g fibre 1.3

Serves 20

calorie breakdown
% protein 2
% fat 2
% carbohydrate 96

Try making another tasty treat by dipping one half of crystallized ginger slices in melted semi-sweet chocolate and placing on waxed paper until set.

Honeyed Ginger Chocolates

Adapted from Buderim Ginger Factory's *Little Ginger Cookbook*

When we were growing up, Moirs' Ginger Chocolates were a special Christmas treat. A few pieces of high-quality preserved ginger dipped in melted semisweet chocolate makes a wonderful end to a meal. This recipe uses white chocolate. Since Honeyed Ginger, a Buderim Ginger Factory product, is difficult to find in Canada, we have substituted honey and preserved ginger for the real thing.

1/2 cup	flaked almonds	125 mL
1/2 lb	white chocolate blocks	250 g
2 tbsp	honey	30 mL
3 tbsp	preserved ginger	45 mL
1 tbsp	cream	15 mL

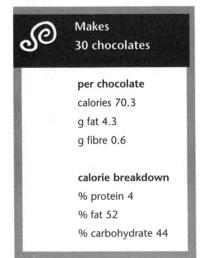

Makes 30 chocolates

per chocolate
calories 70.3
g fat 4.3
g fibre 0.6

calorie breakdown
% protein 4
% fat 52
% carbohydrate 44

❧ Place almonds on a baking tray and bake in a moderate oven for 5 minutes, or until golden brown. Remove from tray and cool.

❧ Chop the white chocolate blocks into chunks, place in top half of a double boiler along with honey, and stir over simmering water until melted. Do not let this mixture get hot or the fat will separate. Add ginger and cream, and mix well.

❧ Spread mixture evenly into a 10 x 3 inch (25 x 8 cm) bar tin, which has been well lined with greased aluminum foil, bringing the foil 2 inches (5 cm) above the sides of the tin. Sprinkle the top with almonds.

❧ Refrigerate until set. Lift out of pan, cut into small squares, and serve.

Although called chocolate, the white variety is actually a blend of whole milk and sugar, cooked until it is condensed to a solid state. Cocoa butter or artificial flavouring is added to obtain a chocolate flavour.

Truffled Ginger

Catherine Metzger of Deity Chocolates produces heavenly hand-made truffles. Uniting rich luxurious chocolate with spicy aromatic ginger, she creates this ambrosial temptation and kindly agreed to share her secret recipe with us.

15 oz	dark semisweet chocolate, cut into small pieces*	450 g
3/4 cup	fresh whipping cream	175 mL
28 pieces	of preserved ginger, cut into 3/4-in (2 cm) cubes	
3 tbsp	safflower oil	45 mL
3 oz	white chocolate, cut into small pieces*	90 g

Makes 30 truffles

per truffle
calories 91.7
g fat 7.7
g fibre 0.8

calorie breakdown
% protein 3
% fat 71
% carbohydrate 26

In the top half of a double boiler, combine 10 oz (300 g) dark chocolate and whipping cream. Fill the bottom half of the boiler with 2 in. (5 cm) of water, and simmer over low heat, stirring frequently until melted. Do not let this mixture become hot to the touch. (If the chocolate becomes too hot it separates into oils and solids.) Remove from the heat and refrigerate until set, approximately 6 hours.

When the mixture has set, working quickly and in a cool area, scoop out about 1 1/2 tbsp (22 mL) of the chocolate mixture and pack it tightly around a piece of ginger. Place on a cookie sheet lined with waxed paper. Continue until all the ginger has been covered, and put in the refrigerator for 30 minutes to set.

Meanwhile, combine remaining 5 oz (150 g) of chocolate and oil and melt, using the double boiler method. Remember not to overheat the chocolate. You are ready to proceed to the dipping stage when you can put your finger in the melted chocolate and can feel neither heat nor cold.

One piece at a time, gently drop the coated ginger into the melted chocolate. Using a fork, lift out the ball from its underside, and gently tap the underside of the fork on the edge of the boiler, allowing any extra chocolate to drip back into the boiler between the tines of the fork. Return ball to the waxed paper by carefully allowing it to slide off the end of the fork. Continue until all the chocolates are coated. Allow to stand at room temperature until set.

Melt the white chocolate using double boiler method, whisking constantly. When chocolate is thoroughly melted, drizzle in random patterns over the truffles. Allow this chocolate to dry, and the truffles are complete.

Stored in an air-tight container, these truffles will last in the refrigerator for about 3 weeks. Allow to stand at room temperature for 15 minutes before serving.

*Catherine insists on using only high quality chocolate such as Callebaut or Lindt.

Christmas Cakes Christmas Cakes Christmas Cakes Christmas Cakes

Mrs. Irving's Light Fruitcake

Heather's mother, Marion MacDonald, traditionally made this delicious light Christmas cake to which we, of course, added ginger. The original recipe came from Heather's neighbour, Mrs. Irving, who was convinced that hand mixing eggs into the butter mixture had to be done one egg at a time and with much beating in between. Who knows whether it makes a difference but it extended the ritual of cake-baking and occupied young Heather when she "helped" Mrs. Irving and her mother make Christmas cakes.

1 cup	orange juice	250 mL
1 cup	candied cherries	250 mL
1 cup	candied pineapple	250 mL
2 cups	golden raisins	500 mL
1 cup	mixed peel	250 mL
1 cup	unpeeled, whole almonds	250 mL
3 cups	all-purpose flour	750 mL
1 tsp	baking powder	5 mL
1 3/4 cups butter		425 mL
1 1/2 cups sugar		375 mL
6	eggs	6
1 tsp	rose water	5 mL
1 tsp	almond flavouring	5 mL
1 tsp	lemon extract	5 mL

All ingredients should be at room temperature.

Pour orange juice over fruit and nuts, and let soak overnight.

Mix flour and baking powder. Set aside.

Gradually add sugar to softened butter. Beat until fluffy.

Beat in each egg, one at a time, beating well after each addition.

Add flavourings, one at a time, beating after each addition.

Mix in fruit.

Fold in flour mixture until it disappears, then fold a little longer until it is well blended.

Pack into a 10-inch (1.5 L) round pan, or 2 small loaf pans, lined with buttered brown paper.

Bake in preheated oven at 325°F (160°) for 2 1/2 hours.

Makes
128 slices

per slice
calories 65
g fat 3.1
g fibre 0.4

calorie breakdown
% protein 4
% fat 42
% carbohydrate 54

Dark Christmas Cake

Adapted from Claire Macdonald of Macdonald's *Celebrations*

Gwen Davies introduced us to Claire Macdonald of Macdonald who has fabulous recipes, including light and dark fruitcakes that include ginger. Christmas cakes improve with age, so start this one in September.

1 1/4 cups	softened butter	300 mL
1 1/4 cups	soft dark brown sugar, packed	300 mL
3 cups	sultanas	750 mL
3 cups	raisins	750 mL
2/3 cup	chopped candied peel	150 mL
1/2 cup	chopped glacé cherries	125 mL
1/4 cup	preserved ginger, chopped	50 mL
2 cups	currants	500 mL
1/3 cup	dried apricots, snipped	75 mL
1 1/2 cups	flaked almonds, toasted	375 mL
2 1/2 cups	all-purpose flour	625 mL
1 tsp	allspice	5 mL
1 tsp	ground ginger	5 mL
1/2 tsp	ground cloves	2 mL
1/2 tsp	mace	2 mL
1/2 tsp	freshly grated nutmeg	2 mL
2 tsp	ground cinnamon	10 mL
6	large eggs, beaten	6
grated zest of 2 oranges and 2 lemons		
1/2 cup	brandy, whisky, or rum	125 mL

Beat together the butter and sugar until the mixture is very well mixed and fluffy. In a large bowl mix together all of the dried fruits and the toasted almonds. Sift in about half of the flour and spices. Mix well, using your hands.

Beat the eggs into the butter and sugar mixture, alternating with the remaining flour and spices. Beat in the grated orange and lemon zest. Mix in the flour-coated fruits and nuts, mixing really well. Add the alcohol and mix.

Pour into a buttered 10-inch (25 cm) cake tin lined with buttered baking paper, smoothing batter even, and then hollow out the middle with the back of a wooden spoon. This will ensure a flat surface when the cake rises. Bake in preheated oven at 350°F (180°C) for 30 minutes then lower the temperature to 275°F (130°C) and bake for a further 2 1/2

hours. The cake is cooked when it just begins to come away from the sides of the pan. Also test with a knife or toothpick. Take the cake from the oven and cool it in its tin.

Pierce cake with a skewer, evenly all over. Drizzle brandy, whisky, or rum over the cake, leave for a few minutes, then tip it out of the tin and wrap it well in foil. Store in a cool place until you are ready to marzipan or ice it.

Makes 128 slices

per slice
calories 88.7
g fat 2.8
g fibre 0.9

calorie breakdown
% protein 5
% fat 28
% carbohydrate 67

Light Christmas Cake

Adapted from Claire Macdonald of Macdonald's *Celebrations*

For those, like us, who prefer the light cake.

1 1/2 cups	softened butter	375 mL
1 1/2 cups	light brown sugar	375 mL
1/2 cup	preserved ginger, coarsely chopped	125 mL
1 cup	crystallized pineapple, chopped	250 mL
1/2 cup	crystallized apricots, chopped	125 mL
1/2 cup	crystallized orange peel, chopped	125 mL
1/2 cup	crystallized lemon peel, chopped	125 mL
1/2 cup	crystallized cherries, chopped	125 mL
2 cups	all-purpose flour	500 mL
1/2 cup	ground almonds	125 mL
1/2 cup	flaked almonds, toasted	125 mL
8	large egg yolks	8
4 tbsp	brandy	60 mL
4	egg whites, whipped until stiff	4

Beat together the butter and sugar until soft and fluffy. Mix together the chopped fruits, and stir into the sifted flour, along with the ground and flaked almonds. Beat the egg yolks into the butter and sugar mixture, one at a time. Then mix in the flour-coated fruit and nuts, the brandy, and lastly, using a large metal spoon, fold in the stiffly beaten egg whites.

Pour batter into buttered and lined cake tin about 10 inches (25 cm) in diameter lined with buttered baking paper. Bake in preheated oven at 325°F (160°C) for 1 1/2 to 2 hours, or until it tests done. Cool in the tin.

Wrap in a brandy-soaked tea towel, cover in foil, and keep in a cool place for 1 or 2 months until ready for topping.

Variation: *Margaret makes a version of this Christmas cake that uses the same ingredients but keeps the cherries whole, the crystallized ginger and pineapple as purchased, roughly 1/2-inch (1 cm) chunks and, for good measure, she increases the preserved ginger to 1 cup (250 mL). She is also inclined to double the amount of flaked almonds in this recipe to 1 cup (250 mL). (For those who like a crunchy cake, the almonds can be added whole.) She also adds 1 generous tsp (5 mL) of almond flavouring to the fruit mixture before adding it to the batter. In our taste-testing experiments, people tended to choose this one as their favourite of the lot, perhaps because it is as whimsical as it is delicious.*

Claire Macdonald of Macdonald suggests glacé fruit arranged over the top of her light fruitcake rather than marzipan and icing, but either, we found, will win raves.

Makes 128 slices

per slice
calories 66.3
g fat 3.1
g fibre 0.2

calorie breakdown
% protein 4
% fat 41
% carbohydrate 54

Glenaladale Christmas Cake

Margaret's grandmother, Laura Slauenwhite, made this dark fruitcake, based on a recipe sent to her in 1941 by Eileen Rafuse, whose mother was a cook at MacDonald College in Montreal. In our version, preserved ginger and dried cherries replaced candied pineapple and cherries; and dried, locally grown cranberries and blueberries took the place of some of the raisins called for in the original recipe. Invent your own substitutions, but keep the same proportions of wet and dry ingredients to ensure the success of the final product.

Makes 144 slices

per slice
calories 90.5
g fat 2.4
g fibre 0.8

calorie breakdown
% protein 5
% fat 23
% carbohydrate 71

1/2 cup	strong coffee	125 mL
1 tsp	baking soda	5 mL
2 cups	dates, chopped	500 mL
1 cup	butter	250 mL
1 cup	brown sugar, packed	250 mL
3 cups	all-purpose flour	750 mL
1 1/2 tsp	ground cinnamon	7 mL
1 1/2 tsp	allspice	7 mL
1 tsp	freshly grated nutmeg	5 mL
1 tsp	mace	5 mL
1/2 tsp	ground cloves	2 mL
4 1/2 cups	raisins	1125 mL
	or 1 1/2 cups (375 mL) each of raisins, dried blueberries, and dried cranberries	
1 1/2 cups	currants	375 mL
1 cup	citron peel	250 mL
1 cup	lemon peel	250 mL
1 cup	preserved ginger	250 mL
1 cup	candied cherries or dried cherries	250 mL
1 cup	walnuts, chopped	250 mL
1/2 cup	flaked almonds, toasted	125 mL
1/3 cup	strawberry jam	75 mL
6	eggs	6
juice and zest of 1 lemon		
1/2 cup	dark rum	125 mL

✍ Dissolve the soda in the hot coffee and add to the dates.

✍ Beat together the butter and sugar until soft and fluffy.

✍ Add the dried spices to the flour.

✍ In a large bowl mix together all the fruit, nuts, and jam. Sift in about half of the flour and spices and mix well.

✍ Beat the eggs, one at a time, into the butter and sugar mixture, alternating with the remaining sifted flour and spices. Beat in lemon juice and zest. Mix in the flour-coated fruits and nuts.

✍ Pour the mixture into two medium-size cake tins lined with buttered brown paper, smoothing batter even, and then hollow out the middle with the back of a wooden spoon to ensure a level surface when the cake rises.

✍ Bake in preheated oven at 325°F (160°C) for 1 1/2 to 2 hours, depending on the size of the pans. The cake is done when it has just come away from the sides and it tests done.

✍ Remove cakes from oven and let cool in tins.

✍ When cold but still in the tins, pierce cakes with a skewer in several places and drizzle 1/2 cup (125 mL) rum over the cakes, leaving them for a few minutes. Then tip the cakes out of the tins and wrap well in foil. Store in a cool place until ready to serve.

✍ Top with marzipan, glaze, or icing.

Raj Christmas Cake

Adapted from Troth Wells' *The World in Your Kitchen*

Whether this cake was a legacy of the Raj or a feature of the rich Eastern cuisine before the British set foot in India is a moot point now. The semolina flour and preserved ginger offer a distinctive variation on an old theme.

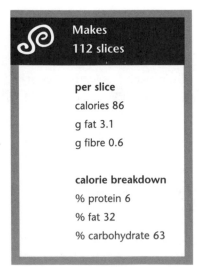

Note: The dried fruit and spices need to be soaked in rum for at least a week before you plan to bake the cake.

2 cups	mixed peel	500 mL
2 cups	currants	500 mL
2 cups	raisins or sultanas	500 mL
1/2 cup	crystallized cherries, whole	125 mL
2 cups	almonds or cashew or half and half	500 mL
1 tsp	ground mixed spices (allspice, cinnamon, cloves, ginger)	5 mL
1/2 cup	preserved ginger, chopped	125 mL
1/4 cup	rum or brandy	50 mL
1 cup	butter	250 mL
1 cup	sugar	250 mL
6	eggs, separated	6
1/2 cup	all-purpose flour	125 mL
1/2 tsp	baking powder	2 mL
1 3/4 cups	semolina flour	425 mL
1/2 cup	sugar	125 mL
1/4 cup	milk	50 mL
1 tsp	salt	2 mL

Chop the dried fruit and nuts and place them in a container with a lid. Add spices. Pour the rum or brandy on top. Cover and leave to soak for a week or more.

When ready to make the cake, take a large mixing bowl and cream the butter with 1 cup (250 mL) of sugar to produce a smooth consistency.

Beat in egg yolks, one at a time, stirring well. Should the mixture begin to curdle, sift in some of the all-purpose flour.

Combine the remaining all-purpose flour and the baking powder. Add the semolina flour. Mix well. Then gradually add the mixture of soaked fruit and nuts and their liquor.

Whisk the egg whites until stiff and fold them into the cake mixture.

Spoon the remaining 1/2 cup (125 mL) sugar into a heavy saucepan. Place on high heat and cook, stirring all the time, until the sugar turns dark brown. Remove pan from heat and pour in the milk, stirring thoroughly and quickly. (The mixture will bubble so be careful.) Add the salt and stir the mixture into the cake batter, stirring well.

Spoon mixture into 8-inch (20 cm) square cake tin lined with buttered brown paper. Bake in the middle of preheated oven at 325°F (160°C) for about 1 1/2 hours, or until it tests done. Leave the cake to cool in the tin for 1/2 hour before turning onto a rack or plate.

Wrap in a rum- or brandy-soaked cloth. Cover with foil and refrigerate for several weeks until ready to eat.

Permissions

The page numbers on which the following recipes appear are listed in square brackets [ ].

Ginger Cheese Muffins [22] and Gingerbread Cream Pie—George Washington [79] from *Kate Aitken's Cookbook* by Kate Aitken (pages 31 and 290). Copyright © 1950, 1953, 1964 by Kate Aitken. Published by HarperCollins Publishers Ltd.

Chicken, Scallops, and Asparagus Salad [36], Spicy Corn and Tomato Soup [29], and Ginger Baked Golden Delicious Apples [92] adapted and reprinted from *Jane Brody's Good Food Gourmet: Recipes and Menus for Delicious and Healthful Entertaining* by Jane Brody (pages 104-105, 257, 516). Copyright © 1990 Jane E. Brody. Reprinted by permission of W.W. Norton & Company, Inc.

Ginger Marinades [8], Ginger Scones [20], Ginger Baked Granny Smiths [93], and Honeyed Ginger Chocolates [108] from *Little Ginger Cookbook* (pages 26 and 32). Copyright © Buderim Ginger Limited, Yandina, Queensland, Australia 4561. Reprinted with permission.

Chinese Chicken Salad with Sesame Ginger Dressing [34] and Ginger Fruit Bowl [91] from *Just the Best: Favourite Recipes from Canada's Top Food Writers* (pages 60, 185). © 1992 Lucy Waverman and Kate Bush. Published by Women's Legal Education and Action Fund. Reprinted with permission.

Cider Baked Apples [93] from *The Apple Connection* by Bebe Ross Buszek (page 176). Copyright © 1984 Bebe Ross Buszek. Reprinted with permission of Nimbus Publishing Limited.

Real Ginger Beef [70] modified from *The Chinese Cookbook* by Craig Claiborne and Virginia Lee. Copyright © 1972 by Craig Claiborne and Virginia Lee. Reprinted by permission of HarperCollins Publishers, Inc.

Wild Rice with Shrimp and Lobster [64] adapted from *Hot Wok* by Hugh Carpenter and Teri Sandison (page 94). Copyright © 1995 by Hugh Carpenter, with permission from Ten Speed Press, P.O. Box 7123 Berkeley, CA 94707

Ginger Pear Chutney [10] and Real Ginger Beer [6] adapted from B. Cost, *Ginger East to West* (pages 152, 160-161), © 1989 Bruce Cost. Reprinted by permission of Addison-Wesley Longman Publishing Company, Inc.

Baked Beans and Fruit [43] adapted from *Full of Beans* by Violet Currie and Kay Spicer (page 93). Copyright © 1993 Violet Currie and Kay Spicer. Reprinted with permission of Mighton House.

Ginger Lemonade [3], Fat Archies [85], and Baked Indian Pudding [97], modified from *A Treasury Of Nova Scotia Heirloom Recipes* (pages 10, 26, 40). Copyright © 1967. Reprinted with the permission of the Department of Agriculture and Marketing, Halifax.

Chickpea and Ginger Salad [32] and Lemon Stuffed with Chickpea Pâté [18] modified from *The Best of Lord Krishna's Cuisine* by Yamuna Devi (pages 120 and 128), illustrations by David Baird. Copyright © 1992 by Bala Books, Inc. Copyright © 1992 by Yamuna Devi, text. Copyright © 1992 by David Baird, illustrator. Used by permission of Dutton Signet, a division of Penguin Books USA Inc.

Ginger Rhubarb Chutney [12] and Lean Turkey Loaf [68] adapted from *A Century of Canadian Home Cooking:*

1900 Through the '90s by Carol Ferguson and Margaret Fraser (pages 40 and 226). Copyright © 1992 Carol Ferguson. Reprinted by permission of Prentice Hall.

Fruit Gazpacho [24] and Moroccan Lamb Stew [73] adapted from *Kitchen Herbs* by Sal Gilbertie (pages 120, 121-123). Copyright © 1988 by Sal Gilbertie. Used by permission of Bantam Books, a division of Bantam Doubleday Dell Publishing Group, Inc.

Lemon and Ginger Spicy Beans [44] and Mango Ginger Clouds [91] adapted from *Ginger: A Book of Recipes* (pages 52-53, 56). Copyright © 1996 Lorenz Books. Reprinted by permission of Lorenz Books and distributed in Canada through Raincoast Books ($12.95).

Ginger Trifle [96] adapted a from *Bermudian Cookery* (page 181). Copyright © 1981, Bermuda Junior Service League, Hamilton, Bermuda. Reprinted with permission of Sheila Gosling.

Spicy Green Beans and Carrots [38] from *Some Acquired Tastes: A Recipe Album* by Jurgen Gothe, (page 101) published by Douglas & McIntyre © 1995. Reprinted with permission.

Scallops with Black Beans and Ginger-Chili Oil [58] from *Hot, Hotter, And Hottest: 50 Fiery Recipes From Around the World* by Janet Hazen (page 22), © 1992, published by Chronicle Books, San Francisco.

Spiced Ginger Cake with Candied Ginger Cream [77] and Apple, Ginger, and Mint Sorbet [106] from *Turn It Up! 50 All-New Fiery Recipes for Cooking with Chilies, Peppercorns, Mustard, Horseradish, and Ginger* by Janet Hazen (pages 51, 52), © 1995, published by Chronicle Books, San Francisco.

Lobster "Chinois" and Pan Fried Noodle Cakes [63] and Buttermilk Marinated Chicken with Bacon, Blueberries, Ginger, and Sage [67] adapted from *Cooper's Inn Cookbook* by Gary Hynes (pages 31 and 38). Copyright © 1993 Gary Hynes. Reprinted by permission of Gary Hynes.

Ginger-Brandy Cheesecake [99] adapted from *Moosewood Cookbook* by Mollie Katzen (page 204). Copyright © 1992 by Mollie Katzen, with permission from Ten Speed Press, P.O. Box 7123, Berkeley, CA 94707.

Pear and Ginger Tart [102] from *Dinah's Cupboard Cookbook* by Janice Poon and Dinah Koo (page 23). Copyright © 1986 by Janice Poon and Dinah Koo. Published by HarperCollins Publishers Ltd.

Dried Cod, Pork, and Ginger Soup [31] and Steamed Tofu Mould with Canadian Bacon [47] from *The Tofu Cookbook* by Junko Lampert (pages 22-23, 40), © 1983, published by Chronicle Books, San Francisco.

Parsnip, Lemon, and Ginger Soup [26], Dark and Light Christmas Cakes [111 & 112], and Marmalade Gingerbread [75] by Claire Macdonald of Macdonald (pages 59, 62-63, 266-272). Copyright © Lady Macdonald of Macdonald 1991. Adapted from *Celebrations,* published by Corgi, a division of Transworld Publishers Ltd. All rights reserved.

Yellow Split Pea Soup with Spiced Yogurt [30] and Rhubarb Fool with Ginger Cream [90] from *The Greens Cookbook* by Deborah Madison and Edward Espe Brown (pages 100-101 and 340). Copyright © 1987 by Edward Espe Brown and Deborah Madison. Used by permission of Bantam Books, a division of Bantam Doubleday Dell Publishing Group, Inc.

Maple Ginger Mousse [96] from *Out Of Old Nova Scotia Kitchens* by Marie Nightingale (page 136). Copyright © 1977 by Marie Nightingale. Reprinted with permission of Nimbus Publishing Limited.

Mussels with Ginger-Soy Dressing [54] adapted from *New Salads: Quick Healthy Recipes From Japan* by Shinko Shimizu (page 74). Copyright © 1986 by Shinko Shimizu. Reprinted by permission of Kodansha International Ltd., Tokyo.

Caramel Ginger Sauce [82] from *Loyalist Foods in Today's Recipes* by Eleanor Robertson Smith (page 123). Copyright © 1984 by Eleanor Robertson Smith. Reprinted by permission of Lancelot Press.

Tofu with Sweet Ginger Marinade [48] and Chinese Noodles with Green Curry [50] from *Fields Of Greens* by Annie Somerville (pages 142-43 and 273). Copyright © 1993 by Annie Somerville. Used by permission of Bantam Books, a division of Bantam Doubleday Dell Publishing Group, Inc.

Fresh Ginger Chutney [11] and Fresh Coconut Chutney [11] adapted from *Foods of the World: Recipes: The Cooking of India* (pages 101, 102-103) © 1969 Time-Life Books Inc.

Baked Pumpkin with Beef and Ginger [70] adapted from *Foods of the World: Recipes: The Cooking of Latin America* (pages 52-53) © 1968 Time-Life Books Inc.

Ginger Cheese Soufflé with Herb Wine Sauce [49] and Ginger Cheesecake [98] adapted from The *Vegetarian Epicure* by Anna Thomas (pages 88, 175, 272). Copyright © 1972 by Anna Thomas. Reprinted by permission of Alfred A. Knopf Inc.

Lentil Burgers [45] adapted from *Good Cooking With Natural Foods* by

Muriel Vibert (page 45). Copyright © 1996 by Muriel Vibert. Reprinted by permission of Lancelot Press.

Oriental Tuna Salad [34] by Weight Watchers Intln. Inc., Tofu with Hoisin Sauce [48] from *Weight Watchers ® Healthy Life-Style Cookbook* by Weight Watchers International, Inc. (pages 111, 199). Copyright © 1991 by Weight Watchers International, Inc. Used by permission of Dutton Signet, a division of Penguin Books USA Inc.

Raj Christmas Cake [114] adapted from *The World in Your Kitchen* by Troth Wells (page 144). Copyright © 1993 by Troth Wells. Reprinted from *The World in Your Kitchen*, with permission from New Internationalist Publications, Toronto.

Braised Duck in Soy Sauce [68] from *Toronto Star Cookbook* by Jim White (pages 74-75). Copyright © 1983 by Jim White. Published by McClelland and Stewart. Reprinted with permission, courtesy of the Toronto Star Syndicate.

Index